STAFF SCREENING NOTEBOOK
10 Steps to Quality Staffing

By John C. Patterson

Copyright © 2014
by the Nonprofit Risk Management Center

ISBN No. 978-1-893210-31-8

Nonprofit
Risk Management
Center
Find the answer here | nonprofitrisk.org

Find the answer here | nonprofitrisk.org

The mission of the Nonprofit Risk Management Center is to change how leaders view, understand and respond to inevitable uncertainty and to inspire effective risk management in the nonprofit sector. As a trusted advisor on a wide spectrum of risk topics, the Center partners with mission-focused, high-performing nonprofit organizations to make risk management accessible and impactful. The Center's products and services help leaders of community-serving organizations embrace new approaches to loss control and risk leadership. In addition to consulting services, the Center develops innovative cloud applications, provides in-person and virtual training, and publishes articles and books covering a spectrum of risk issues facing mission-driven organizations. These resources help leaders free up financial and staff resources, inspiring the confidence needed to take mission-advancing risks.

Nonprofit Risk Management Center
204 South King Street
Leesburg, VA 20175
202.785.3891 or 703.777.3504

Staff
Erin Gloeckner, *Project Manager*
Melanie Lockwood Herman, *Executive Director*
Kay Nakamura, *Director of Client Solutions*
Emily C. Stumhofer, *Staff Attorney*
Arley Turner, *Project Manager*

Acknowledgements
The Center is grateful to Erin Gloeckner for her work as editor of this book, and to Julie Novak, Big Brothers Big Sisters of America, Jennifer Chandler Hauge, National Council of Nonprofits, and Eileen Cackowski for their thoughtful comments on the draft of this publication.

Table of Contents

Preface

The subject of staff screening is a perennially important one for leaders of mission-focused, nonprofit organizations. No organization is sufficiently resource-rich to waste time and money retaining staff who are poorly suited to their roles, or to the organization. And for those nonprofits that serve vulnerable clientele—children, persons with disabilities and the elderly—the high cost of poor or careless hiring includes the risk of harm to clients and legal claims asserting negligent hiring by the organization.

Throughout the history of the Nonprofit Risk Management Center, our team has advised, taught and coached countless nonprofit leaders about the fundamentals of basic and rigorous staff screening. Technological advances in background checking and the privatization of the industry have had a dramatic impact on the aspect of screening that is now considered an essential step for employers serving vulnerable clients. When we first wrote about the use of background checks there was no centralized resource offering access to every state sex offender registry, and most nonprofits obtained criminal history information from their state criminal history records repository. Today, there are a wide range of options for leaders seeking to learn whether applicants have prior criminal histories that would render them unsuitable for sensitive positions. Technology has become fundamental to other screening steps as well, with the advent of pre-employment, psychometric tests, online reference checks, and the growing practice of using social media to gather information about applicants.

Although technological advances have shortened the historically time-consuming process of undertaking a rigorous screening process for applicants seeking placement in highly responsible, risky roles, screening remains prone to human error. Technology hasn't helped us avoid the following, common screening mistakes:

- Skipping steps in the process in order to fill a vacant role or avoid a vacancy following a staff member's departure

- Collecting information from applicants that can't be used for screening

- Relying on resumes, or other information provided selectively by applicants, rather than an application form seeking answers needed by the nonprofit for proper screening

- Discounting the value of reference checks from prior employers, previous supervisors at volunteer service organizations, or even family members

- Over-emphasizing the importance of a "clean" criminal history background check

- Failing to establish disqualifying criteria prior to conducting criminal history background checks

In addition to the missteps above, two new mistakes are increasingly common:

- Automatically disqualifying applicants who reveal any prior criminal history at the first stage of the hiring process, in violation of Federal law and state and local "ban the box" laws

- Requesting and reviewing the personal social media sites of applicants without considering the legal risk of learning something about a candidate that cannot be considered in screening

I am absolutely confident that you will enjoy and learn from this new resource on the topic of staff screening. The book's author, John Patterson, was an invaluable member of our staff for 15 years. During his years of dedicated service at the Center, John was our go-to resource on many risk topics, including staff screening. I consider it a privilege to have worked with John during most of his tenure at the Nonprofit Risk Management Center. Like so many staff and volunteer leaders of nonprofits in the U.S. and around the world, I relied on John's wisdom, insights and practical sensibility. The only difference was that I had a chance to lean on and learn from John on a daily basis.

We hope this book is helpful as you decide how to structure defensible yet efficient and practical screening processes for the key paid and volunteer positions in your nonprofit. By focusing on the right goals, and by thoughtfully choosing and customizing the screening components for screening, I'm confident you will substantially increase the odds of selecting mission-appropriate, dedicated team members to support your cause and programs. Should you require help along your journey, we hope you won't hesitate to reach out to me or any member of our team.

Melanie Lockwood Herman, *Executive Director*
Nonprofit Risk Management Center

Introduction to the Ten-Step Process

M ost employers recognize the tremendous value of smart hiring practices, and the corresponding cost of a haphazard, or poorly managed recruitment, screening and selection process. The former leads to the hiring of individuals well-suited to a nonprofit's mission and work, while the latter results in frustration, turnover, and the need to start over filling an important vacancy. Throughout this book we use the term staff to refer to both volunteers (unpaid) and employees (compensated). Community serving organizations face heightened pressure and scrutiny to demonstrate due diligence when screening and selecting applicants for staff positions that work directly with vulnerable individuals. Vulnerable individuals include children, people with disabilities, and dependent elderly. Their dependency places them at increased risk of physical, sexual or mental harm caused by the acts or omissions of staff.

The evolution of staff screening has mirrored our understanding of the ways staff members create risks for both service recipients and the organizations they serve. Recently disclosed cases of sexual abuse—and the media attention they received—demonstrate the harm that may result when an organization is accused of failing to practice due diligence when selecting staff members.

The concept of *due diligence* is based on a standard of care that in many cases is not determined until decided in a court of law. According to the Merriam Webster dictionary, due diligence is "the care that a reasonable person exercises to avoid harm to other persons or their property." Failure to exercise due diligence may result in legal liability for *negligence*. Alleged failure to exercise due diligence in screening staff members is often at the heart of lawsuits claiming *negligent selection*.

Related to due diligence is the concept of *best practices*. Best practices are techniques that yield superior results for a similar function in one environment and are adapted for use in other venues. Often best practices become the legal standards against which due diligence is measured. In the evolution of standards of care, best practices tend to evolve into standards of care. For example, at one time, conducting criminal history record checks was considered a "best practice" useful for some organizations. Today, performing criminal history record checks is a de facto standard of care for any organization serving children or other vulnerable populations. In most instances, therefore, in a lawsuit involving harm caused by a staff member with a prior, relevant criminal record, the failure of the nonprofit to conduct a criminal history record check would be deemed to be negligent.

Evolution of Staff Screening

Screening applicants for positions in community-serving organizations is far different from what it used to be, perhaps especially true in screening applicants for volunteer positions. Traditionally, when individuals applied to be volunteers, organizations assumed that the applicants were motivated by the selfless desire to contribute to the betterment of their communities. Many organizations conducted little or no screening of volunteers, relying instead on a simple sign-up process. This naiveté was shattered in the early 1980's with several well-publicized cases of child sexual abuse in childcare facilities and youth-serving organizations.

In the early 1990's, a survey of screening methods from 3,800 youth-serving organizations was conducted by the American Bar Association Center on Children and the Law. The study was funded by the U.S. Department of Justice, Office of Juvenile Justice and Delinquency Prevention (OJJDP).[1] The findings of the study were summarized in a subsequent report published by OJJDP in 1998, *Guidelines for the Screening of Persons Working With Children, the Elderly and Individuals With Disabilities in Need of Support*.

The survey's findings offered valuable insights into the screening processes employed by nonprofits seeking paid and volunteer staff.

For potential employees:

- Almost all [organizations] conducted what can be called basic screening of potential employees: personal interviews (98 percent); reference checks with past employers (93 percent); personal reference checks (86 percent); confirmation of educational status (80 percent); and observation of the applicant in the job position (70 percent).

- Overall, 60 percent conducted at least one type of criminal history record check on employee applicants; State and local checks were used more often than FBI checks. This figure reflects a range—almost all juvenile detention/corrections facilities (94 percent) conducted criminal history record checks on employees, compared with only 43 percent of private schools and 50 percent of youth development organizations.

- Fewer than 10 percent used psychological testing, home visits, mental illness/psychiatric history checks, alcohol or drug testing, or state sex offender registry checks on employees. However, 86 percent of foster care agencies reported conducting home visits of prospective foster care and adoptive homes.

For potential volunteers:

- To screen volunteers, 76 percent of the respondents used personal interviews and 54 percent used personal reference checks.

- More than one-third (35 percent) conducted at least one type of criminal history record check on volunteer applicants; State and local checks were used more often than FBI checks. Again, this figure reflects a range. Most juvenile detention/corrections facilities (83 percent) conducted criminal history record checks on volunteers, compared with only 12 percent of private schools, 23 percent of public school districts, and 28 percent of hospitals.

- No more than 6 percent used psychological testing, home visits, mental illness/psychiatric history checks, alcohol or drug testing, or State sex offender registry checks to screen volunteers.[2]

Screening standards and practices have changed in the more than two-decades since the research cited in this report was conducted. The opportunities for these changes were created by a combination of legal and technological developments that facilitate the use of improved screening practices by community-serving organizations.

As previously pointed out, one of the more notable changes that has been made is the increased usage of criminal history record checks as part of routine screening. The use of criminal history records has been driven by passage of the National Child Protection Act in 1993 and nourished by the development of nearly instantaneous and relatively inexpensive named-based record checks on the Internet. What was formerly a screening component for only a limited number of staff positions in a handful of organization types has grown into a standard of care for screening all applicants for any direct service positions. Another relatively recent development is the use of social networks for screening purposes.

Objectives for Staff Screening

Nonprofit and other community-serving organizations are mission-driven, people-oriented entities. These organizations rely heavily upon both employees and volunteers to deliver services to targeted populations identified by the organizations' mission statements.

Avoiding liability for poor selection decisions is definitely a beneficial by-product of a comprehensive screening process; however, it should not be considered the principal objective. There are three fundamental objectives for effective staff screening:

1. Furthering the mission of the organization by employing a high caliber staff.

2. Advancing the goals and needs of the organization by retaining personnel who are well-suited to fill and serve specific roles.

3. Maintaining safe environments for service-recipients and other stakeholders by screening-out applicants who present identifiable threats to others.

In order to fulfill their missions, nonprofit organizations must select staff members with needed knowledge, skills, and experience. In addition, since many organizations are direct service providers, potential staff members must be screened to eliminate individuals who are considered to present high risks for physically, sexually or emotionally harming service recipients.

Screening for Potential: An Evolving Perspective on Staff Screening

"I now consider potential to be the most important predictor of success at all levels, from junior manager to the C-Suite and the board."
—Claudio Fernández-Aráoz, "21st Century Talent Spotting," *Harvard Business Review,* June 2014

Have you ever considered emphasizing *potential* over *past performance* when recruiting new staff? Why have we focused on competency—a term that really refers to past performance—as the go-to differentiator in staff screening? In "21st Century Talent Spotting," Claudio Fernández-Aráoz asserts that the era of competency-driven talent spotting, which began more than 40 years ago, should end.

One possible reason for the default preference for past performance may be the innate sense that past performance is tangible, while potential is immeasurable. For example, we can query a candidate, or her references, for specific examples of how she handled everything from tight deadlines to cantankerous customers. These examples affirm our belief that our candidate, facing similar challenges in the future, is competent.

Yet nonprofits exist in a world of unending uncertainty, nearly constant change, and growing complexity. Is past performance the best predictor of future success in a nonprofit that has to keep moving faster and faster to keep pace with change? And is measuring potential really out of reach for a nonprofit leader seeking to hire the best?

Fernández-Aráoz proffers five hallmarks or indicators of potential as a starting point for hiring the best possible staff to lead and support your mission in the future. These hallmarks include the trait of **curiosity**, which the author defines as: "a penchant for seeking out new experiences, knowledge, and candid feedback and an openness to learning and change."

Few nonprofits can spare the necessary investment in payroll, benefits, training and office space for a new hire whose stellar performance is fading history. Today's ambitious nonprofits need to fill every precious opening with:

- Voracious learners who see on the job learning as energizing **and** personally fulfilling

- Team players ready to put well-worn routines in the rear view mirror and focus on "what's next"

- Confident leaders who appreciate what they know... as much as what they don't know

- Mission-focused people who embrace change and the necessary uncertainty that forms the backdrop for any worthwhile cause, activity or service

So how can you tell if a candidate you've just met—or a current employee—has potential? Fernández-Aráoz advises readers to mine a candidate's personal and professional history, but look for signs of potential rather than competence. "Conduct in-depth interviews or career discussions, and do thorough reference checks to uncover stories that demonstrate whether the person has (or lacks) these qualities. For instance, to assess curiosity, don't just ask, 'Are you curious?' Instead, look for signs that the person believes in self-improvement, truly enjoys learning, and is able to recalibrate after missteps."

What interview questions might be helpful to discover evidence of curiosity? The author suggests:

- How do you invite input from others on your team?

- What do you do to broaden your thinking, experience, or personal development?

- What steps do you take to seek out the unknown?

Before vetting your next group of applicants, consider the qualities you seek in employees. Resolve to gauge future potential to embody these qualities, rather than assessing only past performance.

NOTE: This article was original published in the *RISK eNews*, by the Nonprofit Risk Management Center (www.nonprofitrisk.org/library/enews/2014/enews060414.html).

The Screening Process

The **Staff Screening Notebook** presents a ten-step screening process designed to help nonprofit organizations select quality staff members to advance a charitable mission, while at the same time, protect service recipients, other stakeholders and the organization itself from potentially dangerous or ill-suited individuals. The ten-step process consists of the following:

1. Define the position

2. Determine qualifications

3. Set the selection criteria

4. Create the application

5. Conduct interviews

6. Check references

7. Conduct background checks

8. Make the selection decision

9. Provide training

10. Complete an introductory period of employment or service

The remaining material in this **Notebook** is organized into four volumes:

- *Volume I:* Preparation for screening (Steps 1-3)

- *Volume II:* Information from applicants (Steps 4-5)

- *Volume III:* Information about applicants (Steps 6-7)

- *Volume IV:* Transition from applicant to staff member (Steps 8-10)

The ten-step process systematizes the selection process. Organizations that complete all ten steps are in the best position to discharge their due diligence obligations efficiently and comprehensively. The ten-step process also offers decision points along the way for eliminating applicants from further consideration. The suggested sequence of steps increases the cost-effectiveness of screening by reserving steps that may entail additional costs to the end of the selection process. Ideally, only applicants who are considered finalists for a position should be subject to the most costly screening tools.

Overview of the Ten-Step Process

Volume I of the **Staff Screening Notebook** presents the first three steps of the ten-step screening process. Any staff selection process begins with deciding what duties the position will perform (Step 1). After the functions are defined, the qualifications for the position and the selection criteria can be established. In addition to the specific qualifications for the position, organizations may set generic qualifications that anyone serving in the organization must meet, for example, an organization may have a drug free workplace requirement (Step 2).

After the position description is set, the functions need to be analyzed to determine if the position presents opportunities for harming service recipients, other stakeholders and/or the organization (Step 3). These exposures need to be taken into account in the screening process as well as in further risk management strategies employed by the organization.

Volume II of the **Staff Screening Notebook** discusses the collection of information from applicants through developing applications (Step 4) and conducting interviews (Step 5). These steps offer an opportunity for an applicant to articulate his or her qualifications and experience for a position. The application and interview process also offer opportunities for applicants to express their motivations for seeking the position.

Volume III of the **Staff Screening Notebook** examines the need for information from other sources to confirm and supplement information obtained from applicants. These other sources include various kinds of references (Step 6), licensing agencies, academic institutions and criminal history records (Step 7). These steps are critical "reality checks" since many applicants misstate their qualifications when applying for positions.

Volume IV of the **Staff Screening Notebook** offers insight into:

- Evaluating applicants and making selection decisions (Step 8),

- Following up to meet the selectee's training needs (Step 9), and

- Utilizing an introductory work period as an extension of the screening process (Step 10).

Volume IV represents the transition between the screening process and incumbency in a position. The performance monitoring during an introductory period is the final screening step and should not be overlooked nor should it be unnecessarily prolonged.

Some Caveats

No screening process offers an iron-clad guarantee that a new employee or volunteer will be an ideal fit for the position. This ten-step process is no different. Following a thoughtful process will, however, substantially increase the odds of selecting the most suitable applicant for an important position in a nonprofit. The process will help you select high caliber staff members while screening out applicants who constitute identifiable threats to the safety of service recipients, other stakeholders and the organization itself. However, as is often stated, "The devil is in the details." To achieve optimum results, an organization using the process must add appropriate content and tailor the process to meet unique circumstances and requirements. If the screening requirements are too onerous or criteria too restrictive, an organization may not be able to recruit the staff it needs. If the requirements are too loose or standards not high enough, the organization may place service recipients at risk. The proper balance is a key to the desired outcomes.

Each organization needs to tailor its screening process and content to the organization's mission and to the specific positions to be filled. Screening requirements may look very different for a site-based program such as a YMCA or Boys and Girls Club than they would for a one-to-one mentoring program. Some of these differences will be discussed in the relevant parts of the **Notebook**.

As mentioned previously, the standards of care for staff screening have evolved. They will continue to evolve and organizations must be mindful of the opportunities to adjust their screening processes accordingly. Technology enables access to much more information about individuals that has the potential for improving the applicant screening process. Having access to information does not presuppose that all of the accessible information should be used for screening. In some cases using certain information will violate the privacy rights or civil rights of applicants and could be illegal. Organizations would be well served to seek legal review of their screening policies and practices to ensure that its screening process conforms to state and federal privacy and civil rights law.

Finally, the screening process is not a panacea and even organizations using the most advanced screening techniques must also employ vigorous on-going human resources and risk management strategies to ensure staff members are performing their assigned functions and implementing the policies of the organization.

Common Screening Mistakes / Lessons Learned

1. **Rushing the Process or Skipping Steps:** A terribly common hiring mistake is rushing the process. You are in need of a business development leader *right now*, but taking your sweet time with screening results could give you access to a stronger candidate pool and a better-fitting employee in the end. Similar to rushing, skipping steps in the screening process can be disastrous. Too many hiring teams start in the middle of the process rather than at the beginning—it's easy to jump ahead into applications and interviews, but first ensure those steps relate to the position in question. Take the time to create or revamp a position description that is customized to the skills and qualifications you need in a colleague. The position description is the holy grail of screening—your entire screening process should be built around that document.

2. **Hiring Yourself:** Joel Peterson, chairman of JetBlue Airlines warns that it's easy to hire a person who thinks like you, talks like you, went to the same college as you, etc. Similarities allow candidates to connect with hiring staff, which makes a positive impression. Recognizing a candidate's similarities to your own also feeds your ego, and causes some hiring staff to impose their own successes or work histories onto their hiring decisions. Don't allow your personal bias to influence your next big hire. It's possible that the familiar assets you're focusing on are covering up a quality that make the candidate a poor fit for the position. It's also unwise to hire a homogenous population, or to repeatedly hire similar candidates for a role that has suffered turnover time and again. Invite people with different perspectives into your team, and take the risk that your new hires will advance your mission by challenging the status quo. (www.gsb.stanford.edu/news/headlines/joel-peterson-what-are-most-common-hiring-mistakes)

3. **Failing to Provide Sufficient Support during Onboarding:** Sometimes after hiring a candidate, you realize that person is not well suited to his or her role. Unfortunately some new staff members will never succeed in adapting to their new responsibilities. But before throwing in the towel and letting your new hire go, have a conversation with him or her about performance. It's possible that your onboarding program or training opportunities were insufficient in preparing the employee to meet your expectations. Consider whether the employee has potential to succeed if given more training or support in his or her role. Employment is a two-way street; if employees are expected to excel and give back to the organization, then nonprofit leaders must foster an atmosphere in which that is possible.

4. **Failing to Understand Why People Fail at a Job:** Before hiring a new staff member to an existing position, consider why the previous employee failed or left the job. Recognizing failure points allows you to redesign the position description or to screen out candidates who are more likely to commit the same mistakes. Resolve to use exit interviews to understand why staff members leave your organization. Information gleaned from an exit interview will help you understand the job from the departing employee's perspective. Exit interview information can also help you make changes in organization-wide policy and practice to increase collaboration, strengthen on-boarding, and create a culture and environment where staff feel valued and challenged.

5. **Refusing to Learn from Your Hiring Mistakes:** If you've ever experienced a 'bad hire,' sit down and reflect on the root of the failure. Nonprofit leaders and hiring managers might say, "We never saw it coming!" after learning that a colleague embezzled funds from the organization. But there's a chance that you *might* have been able to see it coming during the screening process. If an employee turns out to be a poor fit for his or her role, dig deep to identify gaps or red flags in the screening process. Did you hire too hastily? Did you skip reference checks since the candidate was a longtime friend of the CEO? Did you assume that a clean background check meant the candidate posed no future risks of misconduct? Did you fail to base application and interview questions on the essential goals described in the position description? Aim to continually improve your screening process by reflecting on your good, bad, and ugly hires.

NOTE: This article was adapted from an issue of the *RISK eNews* published by the Nonprofit Risk Management Center (www.nonprofitrisk.org/library/enews/2014/enews071614.html).

Preparation for Screening

Step 1: Define the Position

Step 2: Determine Qualifications

Step 3: Set the Selection Criteria

Introduction

Staff screening is a decision making process relying upon the collection of information on which to base a selection decision. Staff screening requires collecting several kinds of information: First there is information about the position, including information about the organization. There is information about the applicant obtained from the applicant, obtained from individuals who are familiar with the applicant, and also, information about the applicant obtained from various agencies and databases. Finally, there is information obtained from performance monitoring during a probationary placement after a preliminary selection has been made. All of this information must be filtered through a set of predetermined selection criteria to which all applications are subjected. The net result of this process should be the selection of the best individuals for open positions.

Leaders of nonprofit organizations should recognize that screening applicants for staff positions (paid or volunteer) begins well before they consider any candidates and extends beyond making the selection decision. The purpose of the ***Staff Screening Notebook: 10 Steps to Quality Staffing*** is to introduce a ten-step, systematic screening process that is designed to help organizations achieve their missions while they maintain safer environments in which to deliver their services.

As a reminder, the ten-step process consists of the following steps:

1. Define the position

2. Determine qualifications

3. Set the selection criteria

4. Create the application

5. Conduct interviews

6. Check references

7. Conduct background checks

8. Make the selection decision

9. Provide training

10. Complete an introductory period of employment

Step 1:
Define the Position

Preparation for Screening

The success of the screening process is largely dependent upon the planning that occurs before an organization accepts any applications or interviews any applicants. When filling an existing position, organizations should review the history of the job slot:

- What was the objective of the position when it was created?

- Is the position still needed?

- Have the original objectives changed?

- Has the organizational support for the position been sufficient?

- What has changed since the position was created?

- How should the position change to meet the current needs?

For new staff positions, the primary question that needs to be answered is: "Why is the position needed?" The response to this question should be couched in terms of how the position will contribute to the capacity of the organization to achieve its mission. The planning for a new position should consider not only the duties of the position but also how it will function within the organizational structure. Adding staff positions—even volunteer positions—without fully examining the administrative and functional requirements for each position can be a recipe for disaster:

- Who within the organization will provide oversight and supervision?

- Where will the individual be physically situated?

- What supplies and equipment are required to support the position?

- What other logistical considerations are there?

Both paid and volunteer positions should be subjected to this kind of scrutiny. It is axiomatic that community-serving organizations should not place individuals in positions that fail to further the accomplishment of their stated missions.

Preparation for Screening: Don't Fall Victim to Screening Myths

Sometimes our assumptions get the best of us. This is true even in the screening process, when we assume something about a candidate or about the necessity of a screening method. Safeguard your organization, clients, employees and volunteers by resolving to break down these common screening myths.

1. *"Criminal history record checks tell all."* Most of us feel assured after completing criminal history record checks on candidates, but we must remember that these checks only tell part of a candidate's story: the *history*. Hiring an applicant with a clean record only means that the person has not been convicted of a crime in the past. A criminal history record check provides no information about an applicant's proclivity to commit misconduct in the future. These checks also fail to identify candidates who committed offenses but were not convicted.

2. *"Once we hire a candidate, screening is complete."* Hopefully screening will empower your organization to select the best possible candidate for the role. But screening results are not always predictive of job performance. After hiring an employee, we recommend monitoring performance and possibly re-screening on a continual basis. This may include conducting reference checks or criminal history record checks every three to five years, depending on the nature of the position. For example, an employee who mentors children should probably be re-screened more frequently than an employee who does not work directly with vulnerable populations. You can also re-screen an employee who is promoted to a new position—even if the new position is a lateral promotion. The 10 step process should be re-initiated including conducting criminal history record checks and reference checks from current supervisors and clients.

3. *"The candidate's references will identify any red flags we miss during the interview."* Though reference checking is an essential element of the screening process, you must qualify the reference before assuming that person can provide any relevant information. Be sure to question the reference's relationship to the applicant as well as the reference's knowledge of character, job performance, and job skills the applicant has that relate to the position in question. Even if a reference is qualified to speak to the applicant's suitability for the position, the reference may have a personal reason for lying or for avoiding discussion of relevant information. Ensure that the reference understands the applicant has given him or her permission to provide you with information. Let the reference know there is low risk of retaliation from the applicant if sensitive or disqualifying information is shared.

4. *"This candidate was successful in a similar role at another organization, so he/she is perfect for us too."* While past performance is typically a fair predictor of suitability for a role, don't forget to take your organization's culture and environment into account. If an applicant excelled in a similar role at another organization, it's not certain they will have the same success at your organization. During the screening process, aim to select a candidate who is not only qualified, but who fits into your culture.

5. *"Former convicts make bad employees."* It may not be necessary, ethical, or legal to disqualify an applicant based on a criminal conviction. Disqualification should be justified by the risks inherent to the position. For example, an applicant convicted of theft may not be suited to a financial management role, but may be suitable as a recruiter. The hiring game is becoming more progressive and inclusive, and many employers have chosen to 'ban the box'—to remove the question about prior criminal convictions from the employment application. This allows employers to fairly screen applicants who, though they may have a prior conviction, are otherwise qualified for the role in question.

Position Descriptions

The first task is creating a written position description. Position descriptions usually include several distinct components:

- Position title

- Location where the position will be based

- Supervisor to whom the position reports

- Essential duties

- Minimum qualifications

- Compensation and benefits

The first responsibility for developing the position description is listing the essential duties of the position. These duties will determine the other components of the position description. When defining essential duties, consider the percentage of the available time a person filling the position will spend on each function. If you are developing a position description for a volunteer who is expected to serve for two or three hours per month, there will be fewer responsibilities and the percentage of time available will be proportionally greater for each. A full-time position may have more responsibilities included in the position description, but organizations need to be realistic about allocating percentages of time to these functions.

The duties should be phrased in terms of action verbs. What activities will the person do? There should also be expected **outcomes**. For example, [The staff member] "Plans the program activities for up to eight campers between 9 and 11 years of age." In this example, the *action* is planning and the *outcome* is a program for up to eight campers in the specified age range. Another essential duty in the position description could address supervising the delivery of the program to the campers.

The detailed identification of essential duties enables a risk analysis of the position, and establishes minimum qualifications and performance parameters for evaluation once an applicant is selected. It also better prepares the organization to meet potential legal challenges.

Step 2:
Determine Qualifications

Essential Duties, Minimum Qualifications and Legal Pitfalls

Listing essential duties enables setting meaningful qualifications for the position. There are two kinds of qualifications that organizations may have for staff members. There are general qualifications or expectations that the organization may set for all of their staff members and applicants failing to meet the organizational qualifications may not be selected. There are also position specific qualifications that are based upon the duties associated with the position.

In an international survey of employers cited by the Chicken Soup for Your Soul blog,[3] the ten most identified positive attributes for staff members are:

1. Communication Skills

2. Positive Attitude

3. Flexibility and Adaptability

4. High Performance Standards

5. Good Work Ethics

6. Accepts Responsibility

7. Productive—Quality and Quantity

8. Honest and Reliable

9. Willingness to Keep on Learning

10. Ability to Analyze and Evaluate

In our zeal to eliminate undesirable applicants, we need to avoid thinking the absence of undesirable traits presupposes that an applicant will have positive attributes. The screening process needs to search for evidence of qualities that will bring assets to your organization.

In setting staff qualifications, organizations must avoid violations of state and federal laws regarding discrimination. Federal anti-discrimination laws generally apply to positions in which there is some kind of monetary compensation including some volunteer positions that offer benefits that have more than incidental value. An example of this may be gift certificates that recognize outstanding service. In these cases state and federal civil rights laws may apply. For example, **Title VII** of the **Civil Rights Act of 1964** prohibits **employment practices** that discriminate based upon an individual's race, color, religion, sex or national origin. It's not as straightforward as this terminology implies. In our society, there are some conditions that tend to affect members of protected classes more than the general population.

In a December 2011 informal advisory letter, the Office of Legal Counsel for the U.S. Equal Employment Opportunity Commission wrote, "... because disproportionate numbers of African Americans and Hispanics are convicted of crimes, the use of conviction records to make employment decisions is likely to have a disparate impact on these groups. Where there is such an impact, an employer or other Title VII-covered entity may use criminal history information to make employment decisions only when it is job related for the position in question and consistent with business necessity."[4]

As an example of how this might apply, a youth recreation center is seeking an activity leader and a custodian. The center has a general qualification that requires all staff to pass a criminal history record check. Anyone with a record of any crime involving children is ineligible for a position at the center. As long as the center can demonstrate the requirement is a business necessity related to the essential duties listed in the position descriptions and is applied equally to all applicants regardless of race, age, sex, national origin or religion, the qualification is legal. Since both the activity leader and custodian would have access to children in the normal conduct of their functions, such a requirement would appear to be proper. However, a broader prohibition of disqualifying anyone with any criminal record would be deemed to be discriminatory unless the organization can demonstrate a business necessity relationship between the essential duties and a clean criminal record.

There are some general qualifications that are not protected and may be legal in some jurisdictions but banned in others. For example, it has become increasingly common for employers to screen applicants for illegal drug use aiming for a "drug free workplace." An article in **USA Today** points out that many employers are refusing to hire smokers. "They won't hire applicants whose urine tests positive for nicotine use, whether cigarettes, smokeless tobacco or even patches."[5] The article points out, however, that several jurisdictions have enacted laws to protect the rights of smokers. The patchwork of local, state, and federal laws regarding smoking as well as other employee rights strongly suggests the need for organizations to submit their hiring criteria for careful legal review.

The essential duties of a position may demand that, in addition to general organizational qualifications, the applicant have knowledge, skills, experience or credentials that are specifically related to the demands of the position. These selection criteria should flow from the functions of the position as listed in the position description. They should be adequate to meet the demands of the position but not so restrictive that they unreasonably—or illegally—limit the pool of talent that may apply for an available position.

In addition to protections based upon race, color, religion, sex and national origin, the **Americans with Disabilities Act (ADA)** extends civil rights protections to individuals with various kinds of impairments. Under the ADA, employers are required to make reasonable accommodations in order to employ affected applicants.

According to the U.S. Equal Employment Opportunity Commission's publication, *Enforcement Guidance: Reasonable Accommodation and Undue Hardship Under the Americans with Disabilities Act:* [6]

> In general, an accommodation is any change in the work environment or in the way things are customarily done that enables an individual with a disability to enjoy equal employment opportunities. There are three categories of reasonable accommodations:
>
> (i) modifications or adjustments to a job application process that enable a qualified applicant with a disability to be considered for the position such qualified applicant desires; or
>
> (ii) modifications or adjustments to the work environment, or to the manner or circumstances under which the position held or desired is customarily performed, that enable a qualified individual with a disability to perform the essential functions of that position; or

(iii) modifications or adjustments that enable a covered entity's employee with a disability to enjoy equal benefits and privileges of employment as are enjoyed by its other similarly situated employees without disabilities.

Under the ADA, defining the essential duties of a position is critical as these duties determine the parameters that must be considered when making reasonable accommodations. **The ADA does not require employers to employ individuals who would not be qualified absent their disability.** Employers do not have to eliminate an essential duty in order to accommodate an applicant with a disability; however, adding additional duties to an existing position description could be suspect if it serves only to eliminate consideration of applicants with disabilities.

The U.S. Equal Employment Opportunity Commission (EEOC) investigates complaints of job discrimination based on characteristics protected under federal law: race, color, religion, sex (including pregnancy), national origin, disability, age (40 or older), or genetic information. The EEOC brings action against employers the agency believes is violating anti-discrimination laws, and also negotiates with employers that may be in violation of the law but are agreeable to make changes. The EEOC publishes material on equal opportunity laws and rules to help applicants, employees, and employers understand their rights and responsibilities at work. A wealth of knowledge for employers is accessible at the agency's website, located at **www.eeoc.gov**.

Organizations need to be knowledgeable about licensing and certification requirements for some functions. Wording in the position description may make the difference between requiring a professional license or certificate and being able to open a position to unlicensed applicants. States have various agencies that determine the licensing requirements and qualifications depending upon the specific focus of the position. Counseling is an area that often requires a license. But depending upon the kind of counseling, the license may be granted by a mental health authority or if it is educational counseling, the state school board my grant the license. Some funding agencies or organizations may require as part of their grants that the staff assigned to their projects have graduate degrees, be licensed or have certificates. Organizations need to ensure compliance with legal and funding requirements.

Another area for consideration when setting qualifications is industry standards for specific kinds of positions. Industry standards establish a benchmark for exercising due diligence when selecting staff for applicable areas. For example, a summer camp seeking lifeguards for their aquatics programs is likely to require applicants to have a current lifeguard certificate such as those awarded by the American Red Cross (**www.redcross.org**) or from the American Lifeguard Association (**www.americanlifeguard.com**).

If you are unsure of what the minimum qualifications for a position should be, checking with other community-serving organizations with similar positions to learn what they require may be helpful. Professional associations are also good sources for minimum qualifications for common positions, which may satisfy a recognized *standard of care*. Professional associations are also a valuable resource for best practice guidance when designing professional roles in a nonprofit. For example, the American Camp Association (**www.acacamps.org**) is an excellent source of information concerning qualifications for all levels of residential and non-residential camp staffs.

Assessing Risk

An essential part of the position development process is assessing the risks that a position may create and devising risk control mechanisms to manage the risks. Hiring qualified staff is an essential facet of risk management. Paid and volunteer positions within a nonprofit pose different degrees of risk. The discipline of risk management helps leaders cope with inevitable uncertainty; it does not eliminate the risks an organization faces. At its best, risk practice increases the confidence of stakeholders and helps leaders make the best possible decisions in an environment where it is impossible, and arguably unproductive, to try to predict the future. Consideration of risk management strategies related to screening should be taken within the broader context of a nonprofit's approach to risk-taking and risk management.

Risk—the possibility of a future action or event that could impair or advance an organization's mission—arises from the action or inaction of people involved in the organization, including staff, service recipients, supporters and bystanders. A nonprofit's location or the nature of its programs may also give rise to risk. In many cases a combination of underlying conditions and circumstances create an environment where specific risks materialize. As a result, an organization's screening process must be designed to ensure that the individuals staffing their programs are the right people...well qualified to perform their job functions while at the same time unlikely to present a risk of harm to others or to the organization.

Risk analysis of a position may be broken down into three forensic elements: motive, means and opportunity.

- **Motive:** The screening process should attempt to determine if the applicants' motivations for obtaining a position correspond to the objectives the organization set for the position. Some applicants may seek a position in order to gain legitimate access to vulnerable service recipients, to organizational assets, or for other reasons related to self-serving interests that may be detrimental to the organization.

- **Means:** If an applicant has improper motivations for seeking a position, would the position offer the means for fulfilling the applicants' objectives? For example, if an applicant applies for a position as caregiver for an elderly person in order perpetrate a financial scam, would the duties of the position offer the means to perpetrate the scam, for example, serving as the payee agent for social security or as trustee for other assets?

- **Opportunity:** Opportunities are closely related to means. In the previous example, serving as the custodian for a dependent's assets provides access to funds, that left unchecked also offers an opportunity for embezzlement of funds or wrongful conversion of the assets to the custodian.

Risks to people include risks to the staff member, to other staff members, to service recipients, and to the public. To the extent that your organization delivers services to vulnerable individuals—children, dependent elderly, individuals with disabilities— there may be an increased risk of harm to service recipients.

The risk becomes higher as the level of dependency increases. Dick Sobsey, professor emeritus of Educational Psychology from the University of Alberta, in his 1994 book *Violence And Abuse In The Lives Of People With Disabilities: The End Of Silent Acceptance?* points out that disabled individuals face double the risk of abuse than their non-disabled peers and that half of the abuse of the disabled is committed by caregivers.

Staff screening should attempt to disqualify individuals who present an identifiable risk to others. Screening is an imperfect mechanism to ensure that such individuals are not accepted into an organization, however, there are some obvious qualifications that can be set—for example, if the position calls for working with children, eliminating anyone with a history of child abuse may be reasonable. If operating a motor vehicle were a position requirement, a current operator's license and clean driving record would be relevant. These are risks that once identified can be partially managed through establishment of criteria designed to ensure that applicants with a history of abuse or reckless driving would not be selected.

As previously indicated, of primary importance is identifying staff-related risks associated with recipients of the services offered by the organization. Protecting vulnerable service recipients must be a primary concern of community-serving organizations. Staff-related risks include potential physical harm to a service recipient, to another staff member, or to other stakeholders perpetrated by an employee or volunteer. Harm may be due to acts of commission including abuse, assault, harassment, or excessive discipline. Harm may also be caused by acts of omission such as failure to follow safety rules.

Common Kinds of Risks

Identifying risks associated with recipients of the services offered by the organization in which the applicant is likely to be involved is a critical element of the screening process. For example:

- *Does the position involve isolated contact with vulnerable individuals?* Often, community-serving organizations offer services to shut-ins, mentoring to children, transporting dependent seniors to and from medical appointments, and other vulnerable individuals. Such one-on-one services are extremely valuable but require recognition of the risks involved and have direct implications for the screening processes used by an organization.

- *Does the position require operating a motor vehicle?* A number of years ago, I was talking with the head of a large national youth-serving organization who said that his worst experience was not child abuse, but involved a drunk volunteer who drove off the highway into a river while transporting a child. Both the child and volunteer perished.

- *Are the activities in which the applicant will be involved considered to be high risk or high adventure endeavors?* There are many activities offered by community-serving organizations that must have qualified, experienced personnel in charge. Ropes courses, aquatics, rock climbing, scuba diving, and white water rafting all entail obvious risks; but, what of youth-sports during the heat of summer or construction projects using power tools?

- *Will there be high stress interactions with service recipients, members of the public or other staff members which have the potential for violence?* According to the U.S. Occupational Safety and Health Administration (OSHA), "Research has identified factors that may increase the risk of violence for some workers at certain worksites. Such factors include exchanging money with the public and working with volatile, unstable people. Working alone or in isolated areas may also contribute to the potential for violence. Providing services and care, and working where alcohol is served may also impact the likelihood of violence. Additionally, time of day and location of work, such as working late at night or in areas with high crime rates, are also risk factors that should be considered when addressing issues of workplace violence."[7] Even irate parents at youth sports programs are known to have created risks to volunteer coaches or game officials.

In addition to the risks that staff members can cause to people, they may also create property related risks—to both the property of the organization, the property of service recipients and to the property of the public at large. Examples of key questions to unearth property related risks include:

- *Are care-giving services rendered in individuals' homes?* A common complaint received by in-home service providers is allegation of theft of personal property from the homes of service-recipients.

- *Will the selected applicant be responsible for handling an organization's funds?* Whether it's overseeing the investment of an organization's endowment funds or handling the proceeds of a youth-organization's product sales project, employees and volunteers create financial risks for an organization.

- *Does the organization provide credit cards or expense reimbursement to defray legitimate position related expenditures?*

Not all risks—perhaps even these—that are associated with a position's duties can be so cleanly identified and managed, but any risk associated with a position needs to be considered and subjected to evaluation when developing the screening process for the position. The starting point to effective screening is an accurate position description.

Step 3:
Set the Selection Criteria

Positive selection criteria for any position can be divided into four categories: must have, nice to have, related to the organization's mission but not the position, and completely irrelevant.

- **Must have criteria** are the minimum qualifications to perform the duties of the position. Unless these criteria are met, the applicant cannot be considered for the position. An exception to must have criteria being met before hiring could be made for criteria that can be met within a reasonable time after hiring. For example, an otherwise exceptional applicant for a position as a home care worker does not have a required current CPR certificate. The job offer could be made conditional upon successful completion of the training and certification.

- **Nice to have criteria** are the bells and whistles that make an adequate applicant the outstanding applicant you really want to recruit for your organization's team. For example, an applicant that speaks a second language or is fluent in American Sign Language (ASL) may become a real asset to an organization that may occasionally need to communicate with non-English speaking service recipients or deaf stakeholders.

- **Related to the mission of the organization** but not to the position are attributes that create opportunities for staff development. An applicant that brings in skills in website development may offer a hidden asset to an organization that is looking for innovative ways to reach its stakeholders even though the position may not require specific technology skills.

- **Completely irrelevant criteria** are the clutter that many individuals include in their applications and resumes that organizations need to review but not be distracted by. Often this information is fluff and puffery intended to disguise an otherwise inadequate application.

Just as there are positive selection criteria, there are also negative factors that must be considered in the selection process. These may be sorted into two categories: must not have and proceed with caution.

- **Must not have criteria** are disqualifiers of all applicants—even those who would be outstanding except for this element in their backgrounds. The "must not have" disqualifiers may be set by your organization's board of directors, management team or by the laws of the jurisdiction where you operate. An example of a must not have disqualification would be a history of child abuse for a position involving work with children.

- **Proceed with caution** factors are aspects of an applicant's background that need to be explained or explored further. For example, an applicant who has significant holes in employment history or one claiming extensive employment experience that would be unlikely for an individual of the applicant's age. NOTE: three states—New Jersey, Oregon and DC—have adopted laws that prohibit employers from discriminating against applicants who are currently unemployed. Although there is no similar federal law, periods of unemployment in an applicant's history or current unemployed status should not serve as the sole basis for eliminating an applicant for consideration.[8]

Setting selection criteria should be accomplished when the position is developed. It is very important to set the criteria before seeking applicants for a position. One of the reasons for this is fairness in the selection process—ensuring that everyone will be considered using the same metrics. Another reason—as discussed in subsequent sections of the **Staff Screening Notebook**—is to assist in the creation of the screening tools that will capture information documenting the degree to which applicants meet the criteria for the specific position. Without setting the criteria that will be used to assess applicants, how would you be sure that the screening process will collect the necessary information?

Information from Applicants

Step 4: Create the Application

Step 5: Conduct Interviews

Introduction

The first volume of the **Staff Screening Notebook** presented steps one through three of the ten-step screening process. *Volume I* stressed the importance of laying a proper foundation for staff selection. The development of comprehensive position descriptions enables nonprofit organizations to establish selection criteria based on the specific duties of each position. These selection criteria should take into consideration the current standards of care applicable to the position and the recommended "best practices" applied to similar positions within community-serving organizations.

Volume I also reviews the use of position descriptions as the basis for identifying risks associated with each position and using the screening process as the initial step of risk management for the organization. Selecting highly qualified staff members who are capable of helping the organization achieve its mission is an essential element of the risk management process. Irrespective of the qualifications of applicants, an organization must also search for and consider information about applicants that may indicate potential threats to individuals receiving services from the organization or to the organization itself.

While *Volume I* was focused on setting the parameters for the screening process based upon the responsibilities of the position, *Volume II* and *Volume III* will help the reader develop the tools to collect information on which organizations may base their selection decisions. *Volume II* discusses gathering and using information obtained from applicants—typically information obtained from applications (Step 4) and from interviews (Step 5). *Volume III* addresses obtaining information about the applicant from other sources—reference checking (Step 6), and background checks (Step 7) including checking criminal history records, social networks, and credentials verification.

The **Staff Screening Notebook** offers a menu of possible screening choices for nonprofit and community-serving organizations. These choices are flexible for staff positions that are critical to the organization's ability to accomplish its mission. For positions that expose the organization and its clientele to higher levels of risk, the organization needs to use more of the screening techniques discussed. For positions that pose lower levels of risks, using a less comprehensive screening process may be possible. Until the position description is formulated and assessed for risks, the screening process cannot be designed.

Step 4:
Create the Application

A well-designed application provides the opportunity to evaluate an applicant's qualifications and relevant experience. An effective application should also test an applicant's abilities to follow instructions, express coherent thoughts, and demonstrate analytic, problem-solving abilities—factors that go beyond a simple litany of academic degrees and career chronologies. From a risk management perspective, applications offer the opportunity to select quality staff members and to begin the process of identifying potential risks posed by an applicant to the organization the community it serves.

Applications vs. Resumes

In order to capture the information that your organization needs for making informed, impartial selection decisions, we recommend the use of customized applications. Resumes generally present information that applicants feel is positive and therefore want employers to consider. Resumes may omit information that could reveal weaknesses. Properly designed applications offer several advantages over resumes:

- Applications help to create a level playing field for all applicants by requiring every applicant to submit uniform information by which each will be evaluated. Many employers will accept resumes but also require applicants to complete and submit applications.

- Applications clarify the classification of a position by stating whether the position is considered to be full-time or part-time, temporary, volunteer, and exempt or non-exempt. In addition the application should state, when applicable, that the application is for *at-will* employment.

- Applications should include a statement authorizing the organization to contact any individuals or information sources to verify the information stated in the application.

- Applications avoid considering information that constitutes an impermissible selection factor. For example a resume may state that an applicant was active in a religious sect that held different beliefs than the individual making the selection but which is unrelated to the requirements of the position and could create the impression that an organization considered the applicant's faith when making the selection decision. The prudent course of action is to limit application questions to those that reveal information that can legally be considered in evaluating the applicant.

- Applications also help screening personnel eliminate applicants who do not meet the minimum qualifications for the position, including those who do not meet the organization's standards for employees or volunteers or applicants who refuse to provide needed information.

Constructing Applications

Current technology offers opportunities for organizations to create application formats that more precisely address the requirements of specific positions. The days of a standard, "one size fits all" employment application from the office supply store are all but gone. Many organizations require applicants to complete an online application.

Although many employment and volunteer applications have the same basic elements, an effective application is customized to obtain position-specific information. The standard or basic elements generally include:

- Identification and contact information

- Academic accomplishments

- Specialized training and certificates

- Relevant employment history

- Professional awards

- Membership in professional associations and volunteer activities

- Authorship of publications, articles, and blogs

- Relevant criminal history information* and motor vehicle record

- Professional and personal references

- Authorizations, notices and waivers

These elements can be structured in an application to obtain the information needed for screening applicants for a specific position

*NOTE: permitted in jurisdictions without a "ban the box" law that applies to private employers

Custom vs. Generic Employment Applications

To customize or not to customize? Nonprofits everywhere face this question when designing employment applications. You could purchase off-the-shelf application software with a single application form for every role at your organization, but that option might not meet all of your needs. Or you could create custom application forms—tailoring them to specific roles—which might cause more time and expense on the front end, but save time and costly hiring mistakes in the long term. Should you go for a pre-fab application that only satisfies some of your requirements, or should you spend a little extra for a custom fit? For help in making this decision, consider the pros and cons of custom and generic employment applications, listed below.

GENERIC EMPLOYMENT APPLICATIONS	CUSTOM EMPLOYMENT APPLICATIONS
Pros: • Meets the majority of your needs • Typically faster and easier to implement • Can be scaled up or scaled down as needed; can accommodate numerous applicants • Little internal support required	**Pros:** • Meets all of your needs; can be continually updated to meet new position requirements • Allows for full control; allows employer to select specific information that applicants should submit • Offers applicants a more accurate depiction of the organization (custom application language often conveys organizational values and culture) • Will not become obsolete if maintained properly
Cons: • May not offer you specific, useful information regarding the applicants' suitability for the position in question; may require the use of a supplemental application • Some features may not be optimal, or some functions may be missing • Higher up-front costs; but, costs must be weighed against the potential increase in risk exposure resulting from an inadequate application • May become obsolete over time	**Cons:** • Cannot be scaled up or scaled down—must be tailored and revamped for each role (though this tailoring might be made easier with an online resource) • Requires frequent attention • Incurs costs over time; but again, costs must be weighed against the potential increase in risk exposure resulting from an inadequate application • May require increased oversight or evaluation to ensure that applications are effective and that hiring staff are habitually updating applications

Consider using a hybrid approach to design your employment applications. There are standard items on every employment application, but there are also specific elements of particular importance for each type of position. The investment in time to customize an application for each kind of position is minimal—especially in organizations that have many similar positions. Once the customization is made, depending on the outcomes of periodic reviews, the application can be used for quite a while.

Identification and Contact Information

Nearly all employment applications begin with the items that identify the applicant and provide contact information. While these are basic elements, organizations need to be mindful of the pitfalls of asking for the wrong kinds of identification information on their applications. The following table indicates permissible and impermissible/inadvisable items related to applicant identification and contact:

Permissible Items	Impermissible/Inadvisable Items
• Full Name	• Age, Date of Birth, or High School Graduation date
• Current Residential Address	• Religious Preference
• Residential Addresses for Past Five Years	• Gender
• Landline Telephone Number	• Social Security Number
• Cellular Telephone Number	• Marital Status
• Fax Number	• Citizenship
• Email address	• Driver's License Number
• Social Network Webpages	• Race, ethnicity

The permissible identification and contact items on applications for paid positions are apparent and straight-forward. They provide the organization sufficient information to identify an applicant and to contact contenders for following-up on their applications. The impermissible/ inadvisable items may be legally questionable due to various federal and state employment statutes. This is particularly true if the application is for a paid position or for volunteer positions that offer substantial economic benefits or the promise of future employment to the volunteer. (Most employment discrimination laws apply only to positions associated with economic benefits. However, if there is significant economic benefit from a "volunteer" position, anti-discrimination laws may apply. For example, receiving a stipend or a valuable gift certificate in exchange for a set number of hours of service may be deemed a significant financial benefit.)

Many community-serving organizations collect information listed as impermissible/ inadvisable on **volunteer registration** forms in order to facilitate background checks as part of a more efficient screening process. Most of these volunteers need only to pass a background check in order to be accepted by the organization. Frequently such applicants are parents or other family members supporting their family members' participation in the organizations' activities. The registration form for a volunteer parents' committee for a youth group may include all of the permissible items as well as the date of birth, social security number and, if the position requires transporting youth members to and from activities, driver's license information and proof of automobile insurance. This information is reasonable since it is necessary in order for the organization to conduct a background check. In this instance, the parent or other applicant is presumed to be eligible unless a criminal history record check or driving record disqualifies him or her. A substantial number of volunteer positions fall into this category.

Key volunteer positions should be subjected to a comprehensive selection process. These positions include: scout unit leaders, mentors for young people, coaches, drivers for individuals with disabilities, in-home service providers—including volunteers delivering meals to shut-ins. Any volunteer position in which a significant relationship may be established with a vulnerable individual—child, youth, individual with disability, or a dependent elderly person—should be subject to thoughtful and careful screening.

Academic Accomplishments

Many employment positions require some level of educational achievement; many do not. For many—if not most—volunteer positions, academic preparation is irrelevant to the screening process, but it may be useful in determining how best to use the talents of the individual in carrying out the mission of the organization. Organizations need to decide if requesting information about academic accomplishments is necessary in order to make a selection decision for the position in question or is otherwise helpful to the organization. If it is relevant (or helpful) then the application should request the information:

EDUCATIONAL LEVEL

Did you graduate from high school or receive a GED?   _____Yes   _____ No

Do you have a college degree?   _____Yes   _____ No
(Identify the degree received and college or university awarding it)

    Undergraduate Degree_____

    School_____   Major_____

    Graduate Degree_____

    School_____   Major_____

    Doctorate_____

    School_____   Major_____

Note that in the previous sample, the dates that the diploma or degrees were awarded are not requested. This is a purposeful omission. By not asking for educational dates on the application, organizations reduce the risk of claims alleging illegal age discrimination from unsuccessful applicants. These dates, especially high school graduation, are indicators of the approximate age of the applicant. As the screening process progresses, there will be ample opportunities to obtain the dates of educational achievements and facilitate validation of the information when necessary.

Specialized Training and Certificates

The application should request information about any training and certificates that are relevant to the position under consideration. Because training dates and certifications are not predictive of the age of the applicants, the dates may be specified on the application. If an applicant claims possession of a certificate, the type of certificate, the date it was earned, the expiration date, as well as the issuer should be requested. If the certificate has an identification number, the number should be requested also. Requesting an identification number on the application will simplify verification as part of a subsequent step in the screening process.

SPECIALIZED TRAINING AND CERTIFICATES

Training Courses Completed

Name of Course_____

Organization_____

Dates of Training_____ to _____

Certificate_____

Expiration Date_____

Location_____

Additional Certificates

Name of Certificate_____

Identification Number_____

Date Received_____ Expiration Date_____

Organization_____

Location_____

When using electronic applications, if additional training or certificates need to be listed, it is easy to insert additional items.

Relevant Employment History

The listing of past employment on an application should be more than a simple chronology of employers, dates of employment and position titles. It is helpful to see an applicant's progression and professional growth over their years of service. And while gaps in employment have historically been a red flag to hiring personnel, it is never appropriate to eliminate a candidate from consideration simply because of current or past unemployed status. The relevant employment history section of an application should provide the applicant with an opportunity to describe past duties and responsibilities against the context of the position they are seeking.

EMPLOYMENT HISTORY

Employer_____

Position Held _____

Location_____

Telephone Number_____

Dates of Employment_____ to _____ Hours per week or FT/PT Status _____

Reason(s) for Leaving _____

Name and Title of Immediate Supervisor _____

Email_____ Telephone_____

Please list your duties in this position that you feel support your qualifications for *(Insert the title of the position subject to this application)* _____

_____

_____

_____

The template above collects the necessary information to create a chronology of employment and it also relates the employment history to the position being filled. When using an electronic application, the format may be repeated as many times as is necessary to compile a complete employment history. A similar format may be used to collect relevant information concerning volunteer experience. Keep in mind that an applicant's prior volunteer positions may bolster the qualifications and point to relevant experience for a future paid position.

Skills Matrix

In addition to the use of the employment history template, a skills matrix is a useful tool for cross-referencing the skills and knowledge required for the position with the applicant's education, training and experience. A skills matrix is simply a grid listing the qualifications in the first column and referencing the training or experience in which the skills or knowledge were gained or used.

The following template is a sample of a skills matrix:

Instructions: Please list in the appropriate column your education, training and experience for the knowledge or skill listed in the first column. Details of the education, training and experience you indicate in the matrix should be itemized in the appropriate sections of your application.

Qualifying Skill or Knowledge	Education/Training	Employment or Volunteer Experience

The position description determines the list of skills and knowledge listed in the first column. For clerical positions specific use of the organization's software programs may be among the skills listed. For arts and crafts instructors at a summer camp, specific areas of crafts and tool use as well as working with children of a similar age range could be appropriate. The skills matrix provides a tool by which the minimum qualifications for a position can be evaluated in a comprehensive and efficient manner. Information obtained from the matrix may be used as the initial screening filter. If the minimum qualifications are not met, the person can be eliminated from further consideration.

Awards

Awards may or may not be relevant to an applicant's skill set. Some awards are ego boosters designed to help publishers sell directories of listed individuals. There are, however, awards that represent meaningful recognition of career accomplishments that, when relevant to the position being sought, should be factored into the selection process. Of particular import are the recognitions given by professional associations to individuals for their contributions to furthering an interest area or profession.

PROFESSIONAL AWARDS OR RECOGNITION

*(Please list any professional awards or recognitions that you feel support
your application for this position)*

Date_____   Name of Award_____

Organization Bestowing the Award_____

Basis of the Award _____

_____

_____

_____

Professional Associations and Volunteer Activities

Involvement in professional associations and community activities is often considered
an asset for applicants when the professional association or activity is related to the
responsibilities of the position. Some organizations consider such memberships to
be important enough to subsidize memberships in organizations deemed beneficial
to the organization. For example, a community-based nonprofit may encourage staff
members to become active in civic organizations in order to develop networking with
local business leaders and community decision makers. Organizations employing
specialized professionals may pay for memberships in related organizations thereby
taking advantage of training and informational resources that such organizations
offer as member benefits. The relatedness of the organization to the performance
of duties specified in the position description is the determining factor in deciding
if organizational support for staff participation is justified. For the purpose of the
application, the organization needs to know about past and current affiliations that may
be supportive of an applicant's bid for employment.

The organization also needs to know and have a clear understanding of the extent of the
applicant's commitment and involvement with organizations that may not be related to
the position. For example, an applicant may be a commissioner in a youth sports program
that requires being available to respond to a variety of urgent needs—an official getting
sick, a facility being locked and the teams can't get in, irate parents, and a plethora of
other things that are unpredictable and require immediate attention. The ability to
respond effectively in adverse circumstances is a definite plus, but it is not too difficult
to see that these demands may interfere with focusing on the duties of the position the
organization is filling.

If, however, your organization is seeking a volunteer to serve as a league commissioner, it is necessary to find someone with the organizational skills and the flexibility to respond to urgent needs without risking their paid employment. In either circumstance the applicant will need to balance the needs of the position with other aspects of their life.

PROFESSIONAL ASSOCIATIONS AND VOLUNTEER ACTIVITIES
(Please identify organizations in which you are active and your role within each group. Also, explain any benefits that you consider our organization may gain from your affiliations.)

Organization_____

Your Role(s) in the Organization _____

Benefits to the Organization _____

_____

_____

_____

Requesting information about memberships in professional associations and volunteer activities on the application sets the stage for developing mutual understanding and expectations during the interview stage of how commitments to these organizations mesh with the responsibilities to the employer.

Authorship of Publications, Articles, Blogs

If writing ability is an important job skill, evidence of the ability may be demonstrated in samples of applicants' publications. Traditionally, consideration has been given to hard copy publications. With the proliferation of electronic communications, additional venues for written expression have opened. Blogs may actually be more indicative of an individual's writing ability than articles and books as they tend to be more extemporaneous utterances without being filtered by wordsmithing, grammar-correcting editors. For many positions, publication of articles, books and blogs may give insight into qualifications, professional standing, and ability to organize and communicate material.

AUTHORSHIP OF PUBLICATIONS, ARTICLES, BLOGS

Type of Publication: _____ Book; _____ Professional Journal Article; _____ Blog; _____ Other

Title_____

Publisher_____

URL if electronic media_____

ISBN_____

Topic/Description_____

_____

_____

_____

Even if a written product has limited distribution, it can offer a valuable sample of writing ability. For example, a volunteer who publishes a community association's monthly newsletter may not have "professional experience" but, nonetheless, the newsletter is documentation of writing ability and should be taken into consideration when the ability to write is a qualification for the position.

Relevant Criminal History Information, Credit Checks and Motor Vehicle Records

For the past couple of decades, information databases have become a focal point for pre-employment screening—especially criminal history databases. An ensuing section of the **Staff Screening Notebook** addresses how to access and research those records. This section offers guidance on what items should be included on an application.

It is important to stress that there are legal constraints imposed by the state and federal laws and by court decisions that prohibit some areas of inquiry. In general, organizations need to be able to demonstrate a connection between the request for information on the application and the responsibilities of the position. For example, in California, "employers may not ask applicants to disclose information concerning an arrest or detention that did not result in a conviction. Also, the California Labor Code prohibits employers from using certain types of convictions to determine employment eligibility, including: 1) any record regarding a referral to and participation in a pre-trial or post-trial diversion program; and 2) convictions for some marijuana-related offenses that are more than two years old. (Certain exceptions exist for government law enforcement agencies, and for "health facility" employers hiring for positions with regular access to patients.)"[9]

Because of the variety in state labor laws, it is strongly recommended that organizations seek review by legal counsel of all screening policies and procedures including policies for screening volunteers.

Questions on employment applications pertaining to an applicant's background should be specific and relate to pre-set eligibility criteria directly associated with job functions stated in the position description. The following are some examples:

For direct service positions working with vulnerable populations:

- Have you ever been convicted of a violent crime?[10]

- Are you required under any state or federal law to register as a sex offender?

- Are any criminal charges pending against you for which a final disposition has not been rendered?

- Have you been convicted in any court of a misdemeanor crime of domestic violence?

- Is your access to children subject to court ordered supervision?

- Have any abuse charges been investigated **and** substantiated by a protective services or welfare agency?[11]

- Are you subject to a court order that restrains you from harassing, stalking, or threatening an intimate partner or child of such intimate partner?

- Have you been terminated from a position due to allegations of inappropriate conduct?

For positions giving access to financial or other valuable assets:

- Have you ever been terminated from a position due to misappropriation of funds or other assets?

- Have you been convicted of embezzlement or wrongful conversion of property?

For positions requiring the operation of a motor vehicle or transportation of service recipients:

- Are you a licensed driver?

- In the past five years, have you been denied automobile liability insurance due to driving violations?

- Have you been convicted of DUI or DWI within the past five years?

- In the past five years, has your operator's license been suspended or revoked?

- Have you been involved in a vehicle accident resulting in loss of life or serious injury in which you were found to be substantially at fault?

These questions are samples of questions that are intended to be directly related to the qualifications of an applicant to meet the requirements of a particular position. For this reason, they may be appropriate for the employment application. Additional inquiry into applicants' backgrounds is more appropriately reserved for later in the screening process.

Ban the Box Legislation

According to the National Employment Law Project (www.nelp.org/banthebox), 12 states and more than 60 cities and counties have adopted legislation requiring certain employers to remove the common employment application question about prior criminal history. The effect of these laws is to require certain employers to delay—until a later stage in the screening process—the consideration of prior criminal convictions. Hawaii was the first state to adopt a ban the box law, in 1998. During 2013-2014 seven states—California, Delaware, Illinois, Maryland, Minnesota, Nebraska and Rhode Island—adopted new ban the box laws. Hawaii's law "prohibits employers from inquiring into an applicant's conviction history until after a conditional offer of employment has been made." (Source: Statewide Ban the Box: Reducing Unfair Barriers to Employment of People with Criminal Records, July 2014, NELP). The Hawaii law permits, however, an employer to withdraw an offer of employment if the applicant's prior conviction bears a "rational relationship" to the position for which the applicant has applied. In addition to prohibiting the question in the early phase of screening, Hawaii's law restricts the consideration of a conviction record for the most recent 10 years.

The impetus for these relatively new laws is the concern that applicants with prior criminal histories are too often unfairly disqualified for positions that do not contain criminal history eligibility criteria. Many ban the box laws apply narrowly to public employers. Concern about discrimination against applicants with prior criminal histories is also reflected in federal laws. According to the U.S. EEOC,

> Using criminal history information to make employment decisions may violate Title VII of the Civil Rights Act of 1964, as amended (Title VII).
>
> 1. Title VII prohibits employers from treating people with similar criminal records differently because of their race, national origin, or another Title VII-protected characteristic (which includes color, sex, and religion).
>
> 2. Title VII prohibits employers from using policies or practices that screen individuals based on criminal history information if:
>
>   - They significantly disadvantage Title VII-protected individuals such as African Americans and Hispanics; AND
>
>   - They do not help the employer accurately decide if the person is likely to be a responsible, reliable, or safe employee.

SOURCE: "Pre-Employment Inquiries and Arrest & Conviction," www.eeoc.gov/laws/practices/inquiries_arrest_conviction.cfm

In summary, Title VII of the Civil Rights Act of 1964 makes it illegal for employers with 15 or more employees to categorically exclude applicants with prior criminal histories.

Prior to including any question about prior criminal history on an application for paid employment, determine whether your state or jurisdiction has a ban the box law, and then determine if it applies to your nonprofit. Consult NELP at www.nelp.org/banthebox to determine whether there is a law that prohibits you from including a question about prior criminal history on your job applications.

Professional and Personal References

References are useful sources for information and, while you may decide to check them later in the screening process, asking for them on the application increases efficiency and may offer different insights into the quality of an applicant than is available in the remaining application questions. For individuals just entering the world of work, or for those re-entering the job market, personal references are critical information resources.

Rather than just asking for basic contact information, we suggest that the applicant be asked what information the reference can offer that is relevant to the abilities of the applicant to perform duties of this position. Such information is critical to being able to place the input of the reference into a context that is useful to your organization. We expect that applicants will select references that will provide a positive assessment of the applicant, but it is important to know how that information should be evaluated by your organization.

PROFESSIONAL AND PERSONAL REFERENCES

Name_____ Relationship_____

Address _____ Telephone_____

City_____ State_____ Zip_____

Email address_____

What can this person tell us about you and your abilities? _____

_____

_____

_____

Reference Checking Myths and Musts

Dangerous Reference Checking Myths

1. *Employers may only request a reference from the specific people listed as "references" by the applicant.* **Not true.** There are no laws prohibiting your nonprofit from going beyond the list of references provided by the applicant. To be on the safe side and out of respect for an applicant, consider including a general statement on your application granting your nonprofit permission to "verify any and all information on this application, including performance at any prior place of employment."

2. *A relative of the applicant is unlikely to offer critical or truthful feedback on the applicant.* According to hiring managers who have contacted relatives of applicants, this perception is simply **not true!** One hiring manager explained that, "A blood relative is far more likely than a prior supervisor to offer a candid assessment of an applicant. Uncle Joe doesn't fear being sued for defamation, so don't be surprised if he tells you the applicant is habitually tardy for appointments or was fired from his last job!"

3. *References are the least important tool in the screening process and can be skipped to save time.* **Wrong!** A third-party reference is a far better predictor of future performance than an interview. Research shows that during an interview, applicants often describe attributes they wish to have (the employee they "want to be"), rather than attributes they actually possess. Also, interviewers generally decide on an applicant's suitability during the first 30 seconds of the interview, and spend the remaining time looking for evidence to confirm their initial positive or negative impression.

Reference Checking Musts

Remember:

1. **Reference checking is an invaluable screening tool.** It offers your best opportunity to find out if an applicant is trustworthy, competent, and suited to your nonprofit's culture.

2. **Obtain permission to verify any information** contained on an application for employment and persevere in tracking down people who can offer insights on the applicant's past performance and unique qualities.

3. **Don't skip reference checking** because it's time-consuming and at times, frustrating. Waiting in a long line may be the path to a sweet reward—information you can use to choose the most suitable candidate for a key position.

NOTE: This material was adapted from an article appearing in a *Risk eNews* published by the Nonprofit Risk Management Center.

Authorizations, Notices and Waivers

As boring as they are, there are some legal niceties that should be included on employment and volunteer applications in order to protect the organization and the rights of applicants.

- ***Consent to verify information from application:*** applications should include a statement that, when signed, authorizes the recipient organization to use individuals or information sources to verify the information given by the applicant.

- ***Certification of truthfulness:*** applications should state that providing false information on the application will result in immediate rejection of the application or termination from the position. This portion of the authorization is often referred to as a "truth clause."

- ***Notice of "Employment At-Will":*** unless you are seeking applicants for employment that will be governed by a contract, or your nonprofit is located in Montana, your organization's default relationship with its paid staff is "employment at will." This legal concept refers to the right of the employer, or the employee to terminate the employment relationship—at any time and for any reason—except an illegal reason. In all but Montana, unless the employer prefers a contractual relationship, or there is a union contract governing the terms and conditions of employment, employees of nonprofits are at-will employees.

- ***Full-time or part-time employment, exempt or non-exempt status:*** the application should state whether the position is full-time, part-time, as well as whether it is an exempt or non-exempt position. Applications for volunteer positions should clearly state that the application is for volunteer work.

The following are samples of consent and waiver language for volunteer and staff application forms. Before using these, or any sample resources, consider what changes are warranted due to your organization's culture or practices, and also seek legal review to determine if there are any restrictions on use of this language in the jurisdiction where your nonprofit is located.

VOLUNTEER APPLICANT STATEMENT

Please carefully read the following statement before signing this application:

I certify that I have and will provide information throughout the selection process, including on this application for a volunteer position with [Name of Nonprofit] that is true, correct, and complete to the best of my knowledge. I certify that I have and will answer all questions to the best of my knowledge. I certify that I have and will answer all questions to the best of my ability and that I have not and will not withhold any information that would unfavorably affect my application for a volunteer position. I understand that the information contained on my application will be verified by [Name of Nonprofit]. I understand that any misrepresentations or omissions may be cause for my immediate rejection as an applicant for a volunteer position with [Name of Nonprofit] or my termination as a volunteer.

Signature _____ Date _____

EMPLOYEE APPLICANT STATEMENT

Read the following section carefully before signing this application:

I understand that this application for employment is not a contract and that employment with [Name of Nonprofit] is "at-will" which means that either the employer or employee may terminate the employment relationship at any time, for any reason, with or without prior notice. I further understand that all employment is continued on that basis and that no supervisor or employee of the organization has the authority to alter the nature of "at-will" employment, and the Executive Director may only do so in a written statement.

I hereby consent to permit [Name of Nonprofit] to contact anyone it deems necessary to investigate or verify any information provided by me or to discuss my suitability for employment, background, past performance, education or related matters. I expressly give my consent to any discussions regarding the foregoing and I voluntarily and knowingly waive all rights to bring an action for defamation, invasion of privacy, or similar causes of action against anyone providing or seeking such information.

I certify that I have and will provide information throughout the hiring process, including on this application for employment and in interviews with [Name of Nonprofit] that is true and correct and complete to the best of my knowledge. I have not, and will not, withhold any information that would unfavorably affect my application for employment. I understand that misrepresentations or omissions may be cause for immediate rejection as an applicant for a position with [Name of Nonprofit] or my termination from employment if I am hired.

Signature of Applicant _____ Date _____

Using the Employment Application as a Risk Management Tool

The first step in managing the risks that arise from hiring is to select qualified, quality staff members. The employment application is an essential and primary screening tool that permits organizations to select the most qualified applicants for further consideration and eliminate from further consideration individuals who are unqualified for the position the organization is filling. This initial screening is facilitated when the application is designed to highlight the position-related selection criteria. The first step may well be sorting the applications to eliminate any that do not meet the minimum criteria. A skills matrix on the application facilitates this process.

Applications that appear to have been submitted by qualified applicants deserve to be more carefully examined. It's recommended to use a separate sheet of paper to make notations when analyzing applications. Some states require employers to provide a copy of the employment application to the employee. For example California Labor Code Section 432 states, "If an employee or applicant signs any instrument relating to the obtaining or holding of employment, he shall be given a copy of the instrument upon request." Since most employment applications require signatures, the requirement applies to the applications. If reviewers' comments are on the application, applicants would have access to them thereby opening possible avenues for litigation.

Human resource professionals find that many—if not most—applications for employment tend to exaggerate qualifications. Check the math. How many years of experience does the applicant claim? Are there unexplained gaps in employment history? Do the job titles match the training and educational requirements for that type of position? Perform online searches to determine if publications or other professional activities show-up.

The next step in using an employment application as a risk management tool is looking for potential threats that an applicant could present to the organization or to the people it serves. Any history of criminal conduct included in the application needs to be carefully scrutinized. At the very least, such conduct needs to be explained if the applicant receives an interview. Some kinds of conduct, particularly for positions serving vulnerable individuals, should disqualify an applicant from any further consideration. Organizations must be guided by the position description and essential duties it lists for evaluating applicants' suitability based on risk factors.

Decision Time: The First Cut

After careful consideration of the applications received by your nonprofit, it is now possible to decide which applicants will be advanced in the screening process to the next step. In making this decision, you need to ensure that the decisions are based on information from the application and criteria used are fair and legally permissible. Earlier, we stated that individuals who do not meet the minimum qualifications for a position could be eliminated from further consideration.

Also, individuals who, based on the information in their applications, present unacceptable levels of risk to the organization should be eliminated. Since applicants tend to avoid putting negative information on their applications, risk levels may not surface at this time but become more apparent as the screening process progressed through interviews, reference checks and record checks.

Selecting finalists for interview invitations may be a difficult task requiring the organization to rank the qualified applicants. Interview invitations should only be issued to those who the organization considers the *crème-de-la-crème* of the applicant pool. The good news is that your organization has greater opportunities to employ some really great staff members when selecting from many applicants who are qualified.

If the total qualified applicant pool consists of only a few individuals, it is reasonable to issue interview invitations to all of them. If you have dozens of qualified applicants, the applicants invited to interview need to be pared down to a manageable number. This is accomplished by evaluating the applications and deciding who the best applicants are.

In virtually every section of the application, we suggest that organizations ask applicants to relate their prior experience, education and training to their understanding of the requirements of the position they are seeking. This information is valuable for ranking applicants as it reveals to the potential employer the understanding the applicant has of the position requirements and how their background prepares them for performing the demands of the job.

If no applicants reach the minimum qualification threshold, the organization should first examine the selection criteria to establish its validity. If the selection criteria are valid and no applicant meets them, the organization should reopen its search.

Courtesy demands that the organization acknowledge applications and when final selections are made, that unsuccessful applicants be notified. We suggest that a simple "thank you for your interest but we are unable to place you" is all that is necessary. It is not advisable to further explain the selection decision or to critique the applicant's submission.

Step 5:
Conduct Interviews

In the previous step, the organization evaluates and ranks applicants based upon information applicants include in their application. After reviewing the information to cull out applicants who do not meet the minimum requirements for the position, the organization typically will invite a few applicants to receive interviews.

Interview Overview

The interview is an important component of the selection process, but it is only one of several important steps, therefore its importance should not be overstated and hiring decisions should not be based solely on a good interview. Edward Lawler, Distinguished Professor of Business and Director of the Center for Effective Organizations in the Marshall School of Business, University of Southern California writes in a recent *Forbes* article, "Years of research on job interviews has shown that they are poor predictors of who will be a good employee. There are many reasons for this, but perhaps the key explanation is that individuals simply don't gather the right information and don't understand what the best predictors of job success are. A careful analysis of the background of individuals and their work history and work samples are more accurate predictors of success on the job than are the judgments which result from interviews."[12]

In the context of Professor Lawler's thesis, the job interview still provides an opportunity for the organization to meet with qualified individuals and probe the information the applicant provided on his or her employment application. In order to take maximum advantage of the opportunities afforded by an interview, interviewers need to properly prepare and understand the objectives of the interview as part of the comprehensive selection process.

Interviewers also need to know the legal limits of interview inquiries. A good example of what not to ask during an interview was recently demonstrated by the National Football League when asking prospective players about their girlfriends and other illegal areas of inquiry. What does this kind of question have to do with playing football and winning games? The focal point of the interview as with all of the screening process needs to be on the position description— what is the job all about? While focusing on the requirements of the position, interviews also offer opportunities to explore areas of risk related to the position.

The *Wall Street Journal*[13] offers the following tips for conducting employment interviews:

- Prepare in advance. Create an agenda and a structure for the interview, including time limits. Work with HR, peers and your staffers to develop a set of questions and topics.

- Come up with questions in four categories: fact-finding, creative-thinking, problem-solving and behavioral.

- Consider taking the candidate off campus for lunch or drinks once the formal questioning is done to see how they transition from formal office settings to social situations.

When contacting applicants to set up the interview appointment, let them know in advance how much time the interview will take. If it's for an initial interview and several applicants are being considered, an hour or two may suffice. If it's for a final interview and the nonprofit is ready to extend an offer to the applicant, more time may be necessary and some social time may be included such as a lunch or dinner.

Preparing to Conduct the Interview

One of the first tasks that the organization needs to perform is selecting the interviewers who will conduct the interviews. When possible, the organization should have more than one individual doing the interviews and all applicants should be interviewed by a team. In larger organizations with HR departments, the HR staff can serve as the coach and/or referee maintaining focus and ensuring that the rules are followed. In smaller nonprofits, the Executive Director may have these roles as well as interviewer and decision maker. When a team helps with the selection process, key players include the immediate supervisor for the position and possibly a staffer with a similar position to the one being filled.

When applicants are selected for interviewing, the interview team needs to meet and develop a game plan. The immediate supervisor usually carries the primary responsibility for most of the interview—fact checking, job skills, creative thinking, and organizational fit. The co-worker may be in the best position to respond to questions from the applicant about organizational culture and working conditions—what it's like to work for the organization. In larger nonprofits, the CEO or department heads may not participate in initial interviews, preferring to wait until a preliminary selection is made by the interview team and then stepping in to close the deal with the applicant. Before a selection is made, the team needs to meet and review their notes from their interviews. The strengths and weaknesses from each applicant should be discussed and a consensus developed on the selection choice.

Interview Questions

As suggested by the *Wall Street Journal,* interview questions fall into four categories: fact-finding, creative-thinking, problem-solving, and behavioral.

- **Fact-finding:** these questions arise out of the information included on the application. Interviewers may want clarification of reasons for gaps in employment or specific information about a previous position.

- **Creative-thinking:** these questions are more general concerning the macro-environment of the nonprofit's field of endeavor. For example, if you are hiring a person to be a camp director, you might ask, "What contributions do camps make in the quality of life of the children who attend?" For a nonprofit executive, a question may be, "What are the biggest challenges that nonprofits face in the next five years?" The questions are designed to elicit responses that show an awareness of trends and the ability of the applicant to organize and express thoughts on an impromptu basis.

- **Problem-solving:** these questions may explore past experiences or they may be hypothetical "What if...?" questions. For example, if you are interviewing a financial officer for a nonprofit that receives federal grants, a question might be, "Have you ever had to deal with reduction of governmental funds in a time of increased demand for services? How did you do that?" or "How would you do that?" if it was a hypothetical question. Another area of current concern with a relatively long history would be questions about how to handle incidents of child abuse in youth development organizations.

- **Behavioral:** these questions relate to how the applicant reacts to fairly common situations, the perception that the supervisor is treating him or her unfairly; a hypothetical project for which the applicant is responsible is running behind schedule and over budget, "How do you bring it back on track?"; a fellow employee is making unwanted personal advances and persists after asking that the behavior cease. Some HR experts believe that these kinds of questions are most predictive of how well the individual will fit into the organization. These questions also open the door for discussions about the organization's policies regarding interpersonal relationships, respect for each other and other expectations for staff performance.

Employment interviews should be a series of conversations that are structured to elicit the information needed to make selection decisions without having the applicant experience the feeling of being interrogated. It is important for multiple interviewers to sort out in advance which areas each will address during the interviews. It is perfectly appropriate for different interviewers to ask some of the same questions and then compare responses.

Interviewers should take notes during the interview, jotting down brief phrases as reminders that will ensure important items are not omitted when the interviewers get together and share information in preparation for making their recommendation.

Possible Problem Areas

The following are some suggestions for uncovering problematic areas with apparently well-qualified applicants. They address some areas that are frequently glossed-over or exaggerated by applicants:

- Review each prior employment and ask specifically about the reasons for leaving each position.

- Insist on actual dates of employment. Where there is a gap in employment, discuss the gaps.

- Be sure that actual supervisors are listed on the application and, if omitted from the application, ask for them during the interview.

- If the application asked for academic credentials, clarify the degree received. Some applicants may list attendance at college and participation in a degree-granting program, but omit the fact that they did not graduate.

- Discuss position titles. Clarify whether the title listed on the application was the position held during the entire period of service at the prior employer.

- Use the position description as a point of reference. Ask questions specifically about essential duties, relating them to past experience, education and training.

There are some areas that interviewers need to avoid. "As a general rule, interviewers should avoid questions related to the candidate's race, national origin, religion, age, disability, sexual orientation, marital status or veteran status."[14] Similarly, if the applicant volunteers information that is impermissible, interviewers should be trained not to jot down this information or probe with follow-up questions, since it cannot be used in the assessment of the applicant.

Information about Applicants

Step 6: Check References

Step 7: Conduct Background Checks

Introduction

The *Staff Screening Notebook* presents a comprehensive, ten-step screening process designed to help nonprofit and other community-serving agencies select high quality staff members who are unlikely to cause harm to the organization or to an organization's clientele or other stakeholders. The first volume of the *Notebook* outlines the preparation steps an organization needs to take before accepting applications. Taking these steps ensures that organizational support and supervision is available and that the functions of the position have been fully defined.

Volume II of the *Notebook* offers detailed guidance on obtaining information from applicants. It discusses the kinds of information that organizations need and how to develop customized applications based on position descriptions. In addition *Volume II* discusses pre-employment interviews and their role in the screening process.

Here in *Volume III*, the need for obtaining information from sources other than the applicant is addressed. The traditional screening process includes reference checks, but in recent years, criminal history record checks and checks of other information sources have become commonplace as part of a thorough screening process.

Step 6:
Check References

Checking references is an important component of due diligence in a comprehensive applicant screening process for paid and volunteer positions. Unfortunately many efforts at reference checking lead to mediocre results. The information obtained may be based upon hearsay, be inaccurate, incomplete or deliberately falsified.

Reference checks are generally performed as part of the final stages of staff selection. Some, but not all hiring managers believe that it is a waste of valuable resources to check references on individuals that are unlikely to be accepted for a staff position; therefore, only applicants that are finalists for a position should have their references checked.

When properly performed, reference checking can yield valuable information about the:

- Abilities of the individual to carry out the responsibilities of the positions.

- Personal qualities that will contribute to or present a threat to the organization's ability to achieve its mission.

References may have information concerning the applicant's previous experience in similar positions. References may also have relevant information related to personal attributes—either on or off the job—which would offer positive contributions to organizational dynamics. References may also provide information that could disqualify an individual from consideration for a position with the organization based on past performance or character attributes.

The critical and, at times, challenging task of reference checkers is obtaining pertinent information from references, especially when a reference may be reluctant to share that information.

When you are checking references, remember that the individual providing the information has limited time to devote to answering your questions. The more exhaustive the reference checking

Please note: A positive reference based on past performance is not necessarily indicative of future success in a different organization or role. Conversely, negative information concerning a former situation may not predict poor future performance in a different organization or in a position with different supervision. ANY information about safety related issues including violations of policies and allegations of abuse should be weighed heavily when considering candidates for positions involving contact with children or other vulnerable populations.

process appears to a reference, the less likely you are going to receive information that is useful for your decision making. If the organization sends references a questionnaire it should be as short as possible. Lengthy questionnaires are less likely to be returned and may only receive a boiler plate response.

When contacting a reference by telephone, courtesy demands that you ensure that the call is made at a time convenient for the reference. Either set-up an appointment for the contact or, when the reference is reached, ask if he or she has time to respond to your questions. Let the reference know how long it will take—fifteen to twenty minutes should be ample time to obtain the necessary information.

Explain that the applicant has named them as a person who would have knowledge of their ability to perform the duties of a position for which they are applying. Also, inform the reference that the applicant has granted your organization permission to contact individuals to verify information on the application as well as to assess the applicant's fitness for the position.

Some references may require a copy of the release signed by the applicant before providing any information. You should be prepared to furnish a copy of the release upon request. The release should be on a separate page so that it can be sent to references apart from other information in the application.

Many employers have a policy to give only basic information in response to reference requests. This is to avoid liability for lawsuits when an applicant fails to obtain a position based on information given by the reference. At least 38 states have enacted legislation protecting employers from liability for furnishing references (See Appendix A on page 80 for a list of states and references to the relevant laws).

While each state's specific law varies in its particular provisions, generally the laws protect employers as long as the information is objective, related to the position and free from malicious intent. These laws may or may not apply to organizations that are checking references for volunteer positions. It is advisable for *all* organizations to seek a legal review of their screening policies to ensure compliance with applicable laws—local, state and federal.

There are various methods used to collect information from references including retaining the services of a background checking vendor. Please be advised that when a third-party vendor is used, the reference checking process must comply with the requirements of the federal Fair Credit Reporting Act (FCRA). Employers must use an updated version (current as of January 1, 2013[15]) of the disclosure statement of employee rights under the FCRA. The FCRA requirements only apply when employers use a third-party consumer reporting agency to perform background checks. Reputable consumer reporting agencies should assist their employer clients with fulfilling the requirements of the law.

Employers need to be aware that even when a consumer reporting agency does not perform a complete background check (i.e., reference checks, academic verification, motor vehicle record checks, criminal history record checks, etc.), FCRA requirements apply to the portion of the background check performed by the consumer reporting agency. For example, a staff member from a nonprofit may contact references and the FCRA provisions would not apply. The same organization may retain the services of a consumer reporting agency to perform criminal history record checks for which the requirements of the FCRA would apply. If the nonprofit obtains criminal history records directly from a law-enforcement or criminal justice agency, the FCRA would not apply. State and local laws will apply irrespective of who performs a background check.

When organizations conduct their own reference checks, they often send questionnaires to the references listed on the application. With the increasing availability of electronic communications the reference checking form may be transmitted and returned by email. Sending a form to obtain references is less expensive and consumes less staff time than other kinds of reference checks. When an organization sends questionnaires to references *it is imperative to ask for direct contact information to enable the organization to obtain follow-up information.*

When references return questionnaires, the organization must review the information and follow-up with the reference about any questions or inconsistencies that surface. *Documentation of such follow-up may be critical evidence of due diligence* if future actions of an employee or volunteer become the alleged cause of a legal proceeding against the organization.

The disadvantage to using questionnaires for checking references is that they limit the opportunity for interactive probing to clarify and validate information obtained from a reference. Questionnaires also have the major disadvantage of removing any affect from the information obtained. For these reasons many organizations choose to check references by telephone. Telephone conversations with references allow reference checkers to detect any hesitancy or inconsistencies and to ask immediate follow-up questions.

When conducting reference checks by telephone, it is critical that reference checkers document the information received and that their notes are complete. The organization should retain the notes in its files as specified in the organization's record retention policies. *If reference checks are not sufficiently documented or the documentation is not retained in its files, the organization's exercise of due diligence may be called into question.*

Reference checking includes the following steps:

- Qualifying the reference.

- Verifying information provided by the applicant.

- Probing for additional information to support the applicant's suitability for the position.

- Seeking information about potential risks or liabilities that the applicant may bring.

Qualifying References

Do not assume that naming an individual as a reference on a form necessarily means that the individual will have relevant information concerning the applicant's capacity to fulfill the requirements of the position. **The first step** in reference checking **is to qualify references by verifying their abilities to offer accurate, insightful information** needed to evaluate the abilities and personal characteristics of an applicant.

Qualifying a reference is a multidimensional process. It involves ascertaining the nature of the relationship between the applicant and the reference, how long that relationship has existed, and if the information the reference has is relevant to the needs of the organization for evaluating the applicant's ability to be successful in the position sought.

Relationship to the Applicant

Generally an applicant will name a reference because of a relationship formed by employment, kinship or a personal or professional connection. Kinship encompasses family members including spouses or spousal equivalents. Employment could include both paid and volunteer positions if they are relevant to the position sought. Personal references are individuals whose association with the applicant provides them with a unique understanding of the applicant's character, background and ethics. Personal references may be obtained from others named by the applicant such as teachers, counselors, and spiritual advisors—individuals having knowledge of the applicant because of a close professional relationship. These associations with the applicant do not automatically mean that an individual designated by an applicant as a reference will have relevant information for evaluating the suitability of the applicant.

The length of the association with an applicant may also give significant clues as to the usefulness of the information. It's certainly possible that even a brief relationship may be helpful in making assessments of abilities and personal traits an applicant brings to a position. For example, employment that was terminated after a few weeks due to inappropriate conduct would be significant even with the brief tenure of the relationship. On the other hand, a personal friendship that has lasted for decades but that for many years has involved little or no face-to-face contact may only yield information of limited value.

Position Relevant Information

The next level of qualifying a reference after establishing the relationship with the applicant is to determine if the reference has ***first-hand, personal knowledge of position-relevant information.*** In other words, has the reference ever observed the applicant perform duties similar to those required by the position sought? Or, is the nature of the relationship such that the reference can authoritatively speak to the applicant's character and reliability?

One way of determining if the reference has personal knowledge of the performance of the applicant is to ask for examples. If the position involves working with children, the person performing reference checks might ask, "Have you ever observed the applicant interact with children?" followed by, "Please describe the situation and the interactions." The reference checker needs to ensure that information provided by the reference is based on personal knowledge and not from third-party sources or only relies on conversations with the applicant in which the applicant stated that he or she enjoyed being a coach, mentor or scout leader. Being a friend on Facebook does not automatically qualify a reference.

Even when a personal reference is offering information concerning the applicant's character, having examples upon which to base the appraisal is useful. For example, a character reference may state that the applicant is always punctual. Ask references to give examples of times the applicant demonstrated his or her commitment to punctuality that were observed by the reference. Arguably, some virtues, such as punctuality, can become a negative if the applicant is compulsive about them and examples can help the reference checker weigh how the behavior fits the needs of the position.

Verifying Information Provided By Applicant

Once the reference is qualified, the next task of the record checker is to use the reference to verify information received from application forms and interviews. This task needs to be performed without referring to the information given by the applicant. ***Reference checkers should not offer the answers to the questions being asked.*** For example, asking the question, "Why did the applicant leave your organization?" is better than asking, "The applicant said he left your organization due to a family illness. Is this correct?"

Because most individuals named as references will not be able to verify all of the information provided by the applicant, questions should be tailored to specific information from each reference—be it employment/volunteer experience or character traits.

Employment/Volunteer Service

There are many challenges to obtaining useful information from past or present employers and from organizations in which an applicant has volunteer experience related to the functions of the position being sought.

Information from Employers

Many employers will be reluctant to share more than basic information:

- Verification of employment

- Dates of employment

- Major job responsibilities

- Final salary

Most often, when responding to written requests for employment references, the forms will be routed to the HR department for retrieval from HR files. According to Susan M. Heathfield, a management and organizational development consultant specializing in human resources, more in-depth—useful—information may be obtained from immediate supervisors through less formal telephone conversations.

Information about Relevant Volunteer Service

Often, obtaining reliable information concerning an applicant's relevant past volunteer service is more difficult than checking past employment. Information about past volunteer service is likely to be most useful for organizations filling volunteer positions but is also relevant for some paid positions. References from past experiences working with children and the disabled are *critical elements of the screening process when selecting anyone applying to work with these vulnerable populations.*

When the applicant has past experience in a local branch of a national organization and is applying for a volunteer position in a different branch of the same organization, it is essential to check with the local branch in which the person served to determine if the volunteer would be accepted back or if there were problems. There have been numerous instances where nonprofits have accepted at face value statements by applicants that they volunteered with local chapters of various national groups. If these claims had been checked by the chapter the individual was attempting to affiliate with, past misdeeds would have been discovered and clientele would have been safer.

One of the challenges of obtaining information about volunteer service is finding someone who has first-hand knowledge about the applicant's performance as a volunteer. Consider the following scenarios:

- Joe Smith is applying to be a volunteer youth sport coach. He states that he has served as a coach in a similar organization where he used to live. The person Joe lists as his reference was also a volunteer and is no longer with the organization. The reference has moved and is not able to be contacted to verify Joe's service. The organization has a very small paid staff and does not keep files on individual volunteers.

- Mary Jones is applying to be a mentor with an in-school program. Mary states that she was a volunteer ten years ago in the children's unit of the local hospital. She stated on her application that she ceased volunteering when her first child was born and now that all of her children are in school she is ready to make a contribution to her community again. The hospital only retains records on volunteers for seven years.

- John Brown has been recruited to be an instructor in his church's youth ministry program. As part of the recruitment process, John's past experience with children must be verified. John is in the military and has traveled extensively. He has lived in several countries and says that wherever he lived, he felt a duty to volunteer—often with youth programs. He has listed volunteer experience in five different countries.

Each of the above scenarios offers an example of difficulties faced by community-serving organizations attempting to perform due diligence by contacting references to verify relevant volunteer experience and assess possible risks that an applicant may present to the organization and populations it serves.

Document Efforts to Obtain References

Unfortunately, many community-serving organizations maintain only basic information on their volunteer workforce and much of the information that has been collected may not be accessible. When checking references for positions that involve direct contact with children, **organizations must make good-faith efforts to verify relevant past experience.** When an organization cannot obtain the necessary information from a primary source, ask the applicant for alternative sources of information. For example, if a sports program does not maintain records on individual coaches, ask the applicant for a contact that could verify his or her service—perhaps a parent of a team member. **The efforts to obtain information about experience working with vulnerable populations should be fully documented.** If an applicant's past service cannot be verified, note the reason. **If too much information cannot be verified, the organization may not be able to accept the applicant.**

Reality Checks

In addition to verifying the relationship and tenure of the applicant with the reference, information is needed to compare the job title and duties performed by the applicant with the actual title and responsibilities of the former position. An article in the March 14, 2008 edition of *The Washington Post* noted that "Background checks have shown that around 50 percent of job-seekers put some sort of false information on their applications."

In addition to inflating qualifications and experience, applicants may omit information that they feel would detract from their chances to be selected for a position. Careful questioning of references may fill in any gaps in the information supplied by applicants on their applications and during interviews.

Recap: Keys to Reference Checking

- Decide what information you need from the applicants to verify their abilities to perform the duties of the position and meet the organization's qualifications for employment.

- Develop a standard list of questions for references designed to obtain the required information.

- Contact qualified references by telephone or by using a questionnaire. (Do not limit reference checks to individuals designated as references— contact anyone who may have useful information.)

- Record information obtained from contacting references.

- Perform reference checks only on individuals who appear to meet the necessary qualifications and for whom a placement offer will be made.

- If a vendor is retained for performing reference checks, ensure that the provisions of the FCRA are strictly followed.

Step 7:
Conduct Background Checks

The advent of the Internet heralded a giant step in the amount of easily available information concerning applicants for paid and volunteer positions. New industries have been created to collect and disseminate or sell information about individuals for various purposes, including pre-employment screening. With easier access to information, employers have also experienced increased legal pressure to use the information as part of their screening processes. This is particularly true in the area of direct service positions related to vulnerable populations where negligent selection may be perceived to be more easily proven in lawsuits against employers if relevant record checks are not performed.

The flip-side of liability for failure to adequately perform background checks is liability created by violating the privacy of applicants. Nonprofits can face significant legal exposure if well-intentioned but improperly performed background checks violate the privacy of the applicants. Community-serving organizations are well advised to conduct the necessary background checks but to do so with a great deal of care and transparency. Inform all applicants early on about the background checks to be used and seek the applicants' authorizations. When an organization receives information subsequent to a background check, it must handle it with utmost sensitivity and safe-guard its confidentiality.

A key to maintaining the proper balance between obtaining the information needed to make informed selection decisions and protecting applicant privacy rights is to focus the records checks on the qualifications established by the nonprofit for the specific position as well as general qualifications set by the nonprofit for all positions in the organization. The selection criteria should be established before screening any applicants in order to ensure that all applicants are evaluated by the same measures.

Selection criteria need to be established as part of the planning for the positions being filled by the organization, however, the actual record checks only need to be performed on a relative few applicants—those whom the nonprofit considers "finalists" for a position. This is especially true of paid positions. Some national youth-serving organizations require criminal history record checks of all adult volunteers before accepting their participation in any of the organizations' programs.

Record checks are relatively expensive and when performed by a consumer reporting agency may create legal obstacles to making timely selections. It is best to wait to perform record checks until the nonprofit is ready to make an offer. Conduct the record checks as a final step before making the offer.

Record Check Types

Most record checks used by nonprofits are name-based requiring an applicant's name, date of birth and Social Security number. These three pieces of data are used by consumer reporting agencies to associate records that are searched with the individual to which the records pertain. These same items are often employed by identity thieves and therefore custodians of records containing this information must set up reasonable security systems. When using name-based record checks, nonprofits should require applicants to provide a government issued, picture ID with the applicant's name and date of birth. While this is not a fool-proof method of identity verification, it does document recognition of the individual by that name by the agency issuing the identification.

There are numerous record checks that may be useful in the screening process. These are discussed in the following sections:

- Social Security number verification

- Criminal history record checks

- Driving records

- Credential and employment verification

- Residency status

- Social Network and Internet Searches

Social Security Number Verification

The Social Security number is one of three pieces of information used as identifiers when making name-based record checks. Background checking vendors use credit records to verify the Social Security number, matching it with a name and date of birth. This verification does not require a complete credit check but usually yields a record of addresses as well as the name associated with that social security number. The Social Security number is as close to a unique identifier as there is other than fingerprints and DNA. Because it is not a biometric measure, it maybe falsified in an attempt to avoid being identified or when one is assuming another individual's identity.

The Social Security Administration offers employers a verification website for the purpose of verifying SSNs for paid employees *after* they have been hired. Because the SSN has become a commonly used identification for various sorts of business and government transactions it is included in many different databases including those maintained by consumer reporting organizations. Verification of an applicant's Social Security number for the purposes of conducting background checks should be included in any name-based record check.

Organizations requiring applicants to provide their Social Security numbers are responsible for the security of records that include these numbers. Miriam Wugmeister and Nathan Taylor of Morrison Foerster (**www.mofo.com**) report that more than 30 states have adopted laws limiting how Social Security numbers ("SSNs") can be collected, used, and disclosed. Six of those states have adopted provisions that specifically require organizations to develop policies to safeguard SSNs. These states are: Connecticut, Massachusetts, Michigan, New Mexico, New York, and Texas.[16] For example, New York has enacted state laws that carry heavy penalties for wrongful use of Social Security numbers. Under New York state law section 399-ddd(4), "Any person, firm, partnership, association or corporation having possession of the Social Security account number of any individual shall, to the extent that such number is maintained for the conduct of business or trade, take reasonable measures to ensure that no officer or employee has access to such number for any purpose other than for a legitimate or necessary purpose related to the conduct of such business or trade and provide safeguards necessary or appropriate to preclude unauthorized access to the Social Security account number and to protect the confidentiality of such number."

Wugmeister and Taylor advise that "a business must implement and maintain policies and procedures (its "SSN protection policy") that:

- protect the confidentiality and security of SSNs

- prohibit the unlawful disclosure of SSNs

- limit access to SSNs, including limiting access to SSNs to those employees who need such access to perform their job-related duties

- document when employees can keep, access, and transport SSNs outside of business premises

- provide for the proper disposal of SSNs

- provide penalties for violations of the SSN protection policy

Moreover, a business must describe, in its SSN protection policy, how the business collects SSNs and how and when the business uses SSNs."[17]

Due to differences in each state's laws regarding use and security of Social Security numbers, nonprofits should seek legal guidance when formulating and implementing policies regarding use of Social Security numbers for screening purposes.

Criminal History Record Checks

"Review of crime reports indicate that in 2007, law enforcement agencies in the United States made over 14 million arrests, and that as of December 31, 2006, over 81 million criminal history records were contained in State criminal history repositories. Due to the increase in automation, by the end of 2006, about 91 percent of these criminal history records were electronically accessible. This situation has increased the ability of employers and others to conduct criminal background checks on potential employees and individuals. At the same time, the increased access to criminal history records means that individuals who have led a 'clean' life since their arrest, may be faced with hardships in finding employment."[18]

Before discussing the specific kinds of criminal history record checks and their strengths and weaknesses, it is important to consider the role of criminal history records as part of comprehensive screening and risk management processes.

The National Committee for the Prevention of Elder Abuse in an article titled, *What Can We Learn from Criminal Background Checks?* pointed out, "When the records of prospective in-home support service workers in one California county were checked, over 15 percent were found to have criminal records. In Texas, where certain convictions bar employment in long-term care and home health care settings, 9 percent of applicants in 2000 were found to have convictions. Last year, [2000] when New Jersey passed legislation requiring all home care workers to have FBI fingerprint checks, four hundred current employees, some of whom had been working for years, were found to have committed disqualifying crimes."[19]

In 2012, a major provider of criminal history record checks for nonprofits, LexisNexis, reported that of the 5.5 million volunteer and employee background checks performed by LexisNexis for nonprofit organizations between 2007 and 2011, 479,000 individuals were identified "with criminal convictions [that] included:

- 91,607 drug-related offenses, including possession and distribution

- 10,438 sex-related offenses

- 1,178 murder offenses

- 1,021 registered sex offenders

- 603 kidnapping offenses"[20]

It appears clear from the information cited in the previous paragraphs, that criminal history record checks are effective in identifying individuals who have had significant contact with the criminal justice system. It is much less clear what implication past criminal behavior has on future behavior. We do have an idea of how obtaining criminal history records effects employer decision making.

In order to ensure that criminal record checks are fair and a business necessity, the courts have established criteria that limit an employer's discretion cited in the EEOC's Enforcement Guidance bulletin:

"In a case involving a criminal record exclusion, the Eighth Circuit in its 1975 *Green v. Missouri Pacific Railroad* decision, held that it was discriminatory under Title VII for an employer to "follow the policy of disqualifying for employment any applicant with a conviction for any crime other than a minor traffic offense." The Eighth Circuit identified three factors (the "Green factors") that were relevant to assessing whether an exclusion is job related for the position in question and consistent with business necessity:

1. The nature and gravity of the offense or conduct

2. The time that has passed since the offense or conduct and/or completion of the sentence

3. The nature of the job held or sought

"In 2007, the Third Circuit in *El v. Southeastern Pennsylvania Transportation Authority* developed the statutory analysis in greater depth. Douglas El challenged SEPTA's policy of excluding everyone ever convicted of a violent crime from the job of paratransit driver. El, a 55 year-old African American paratransit driver-trainee, was terminated from employment when SEPTA learned of his conviction for second-degree murder years earlier; the conviction involved a gang fight when he was 15 years old and was his only disqualifying offense under SEPTA's policy. The Third Circuit expressed "reservations" about a policy such as SEPTA's (exclusion for all violent crimes, no matter how long ago they were committed) "in the abstract."

"Applying Supreme Court precedent, the El court observed that some level of risk is inevitable in all hiring, and that, "[in] a broad sense, hiring policies . . . ultimately concern the management of risk." Recognizing that assessing such risk is at the heart of criminal record exclusions, the Third Circuit concluded that Title VII requires employers to justify criminal record exclusions by demonstrating that they "accurately distinguish between applicants [who] pose an unacceptable level of risk and those [who] do not."

"The Third Circuit affirmed summary judgment for SEPTA, but stated that the outcome of the case might have been different if Mr. El had, "for example, hired an expert who testified that there is a time at which a former criminal is no longer any more likely to recidivate than the average person, . . . [so] there would be a factual question for the jury to resolve." The Third Circuit reasoned, however, that the recidivism evidence presented by SEPTA's experts, in conjunction with the nature of the position at issue—paratransit driver-trainee with unsupervised access to vulnerable adults—required the employer to exercise the utmost care."[21]

State laws differ broadly on how employers may use criminal history record information. For additional information on this important topic, consult the U.S. Chamber of Commerce website summary of each state's laws pertaining to employer use of criminal history records (**www.uschambersmallbusinessnation.com/toolkits/guide/P05_1600**).

The most common record check in use by nonprofit organizations is a criminal history record check. However, not all criminal history record checks are the same. Variables include: identifiers, jurisdictions, included time spans, record sources, frequency of database updates, types of offenses, and age of offender. Cost factors and timeliness of the results are additional considerations. Nonprofits using criminal history records as part of a screening process need to understand the strengths and weaknesses of their specific approach to criminal history record checks. All should keep in mind that no single criminal history record check is going to guarantee the nonprofit will obtain the information needed to make the best screening decision. Every source of criminal history records has deficiencies—some of which are unavoidable—including cases that have not reached a final disposition, incomplete information submitted to the records' repository, human error with data entry, and falsification of information.

Fingerprint-based Record Checks

At the upper end of criminal history record checks are record checks using biometric identifiers, the most common of which are fingerprints. The National Child Protection Act of 1993 (NCPA), Public Law 103-209, as amended by the Volunteers for Children Act (VCA), Public Law 105-251 (Section 221 and 222 of the Crime Identification Technology Act of 1998), authorizes certain nongovernmental organizations to conduct a fingerprint based national criminal history record check to determine an individual's fitness to care for the safety and well-being of children, the elderly and people with disabilities. This federal law allows organizations, designated as a qualified entity, to make a fitness determination based on national criminal history record information provided by the Federal Bureau of Investigation (FBI) through each state's identification bureau (SIB).[22] A current list of each state's identification bureau is included on the FBI's website.[23]

Despite the encouragement offered by the federal legislation, fingerprint-based criminal history record checks are utilized by fewer nonprofits than other kinds of record checks. The factors that appear to limit their use include the physical necessity of obtaining the fingerprints—requiring organizations to submit two complete readable sets of fingerprints on an approved fingerprint card or alternatively having the applicant go to an agency with a computer capable of electronically transmitting the fingerprints to the SIB.

The cost of fingerprint-based record checks also appears to inhibit their use by organizations with limited budgets as does the time required for processing and receiving the results.

According to a 2010 report from SEARCH, Inc., costs for non-criminal justice fingerprint based record checks range from $5 in Pennsylvania to $75 in New York. The average cost for volunteers for fingerprint record checks through the state identification bureaus was from $19.37 to $23.36, the difference being whether the fingerprints were retained. Some states offer "rap back" programs.

Name-Based Record Checks

Most nonprofits rely upon name-based record checks for staff screening. Name-based record checks are similar to criminal history record checks performed by state identification bureaus for non-criminal justice purposes. In addition, information in sex offender and state child abuse registries is name-based. Criminal history record checks by private vendors are also name-based.

Sex Offender Registries

Sex offender registries are another information source used by nonprofits to screen staff members. Sex offender registries are of limited usefulness for

> **Rap back:** A "rap back" or "hit notice" program will inform an employer or other designated entity when an individual who has undergone a fingerprint-based background check, and whose fingerprints are retained by a criminal history repository after the check, is subsequently arrested. His or her fingerprints, obtained after the arrest, are matched against a database that contains the fingerprints that were initially submitted. Employers are then notified of the individual's arrest. Employers pay a fee for the service in some states; other states provide the service for free.[24] Not surprisingly, fingerprint-based record checks are most often used in jurisdictions in which they are required by law for certain kinds of paid and volunteer positions.

screening applicants as they list only individuals convicted of a sex related crime. Some offenders may avoid being listed by entering a guilty plea to a non-sex related crime. For example, an individual may have been arrested for sexual assault and pled guilty to simple assault. Another limit to sex offender registries is that some positions require screening for other job-related offenses, for example, DUIs of applicants for volunteer drivers will not show up on a check of sex offender registries.

While sex offender registries should not be the primary screening device, they certainly should not be overlooked. The U.S. Department of Justice has made it very easy to access information from sex offender registries maintained by jurisdictions throughout the country through the National Sex Offender Public Website (NSOPW). According to the website, "[the] NSOPW (**www.nsopw.gov/en-US/Home/About**) is the only U.S. government website that links public state, territorial, and tribal sex offender registries from one national search site. Parents, employers, and other concerned residents can utilize the website's search tool to identify location information on sex offenders residing, working, and attending school not only in their own neighborhoods but in other nearby states and communities."

Child Abuse Registries

Most states maintain a central registry of individuals who are suspected of child abuse as defined by that state's child abuse laws. Access to the information contained in the registry's records is limited by law to law enforcement and child welfare personnel. Some states require organizations to check child abuse registries as part of the screening process for camp staff, school teachers, and other caregivers for children. A few states permit access only by these entities for the purpose of screening individuals responsible for the care and well-being of children. Certainly any organization offering care for children should consider child abuse registry checks.

Each state's requirements for access to their registry are established by that state's laws. The Texas Department of Family Services website (**www.dfps.state.tx.us/child_care/ Other_Child_care_Information/abuse_registry.asp**) provides a useful table with contact information for each state's child abuse registry and linkages for any special forms required. The U.S. Department of Health and Human Services' Child Welfare Information Gateway offers a search function for looking at each state's child abuse statutes at (**www.childwelfare.gov/systemwide/laws_policies/state/**).

Criminal History Record Checks by Vendors

Possibly the most common use of name-based record checks is criminal record checks performed by consumer reporting vendors. In the past decade the number of such firms has burgeoned, their growth driven by demand for more information about job applicants and facilitation of access to the information afforded by the Internet.

Nonprofits need to exercise a great deal of care when selecting a vendor to perform criminal history record checks. Vendors should ensure compliance with the Fair Credit Reporting Act (FCRA) as it applies to consumer reports. In this regard, before establishing a relationship with a vendor, the nonprofit should review with the vendor its FCRA compliance procedures and the assistance it offers to the employer to meet its compliance requirements.

How the screening firm acquires its criminal history information is important too. There are three main methods for getting this data, and many firms use a combination of the three: using their own in-house researchers, contracting local court retrieval service companies to go to the courts for them, and doing database searches. "It's important for the HR industry to ferret out those who use databases. If a screening firm is relying on third-party databases to conduct criminal history record checks, employers should ask if the court sanctions the database and how often the material is updated."[25]

Private companies maintain databases that typically contain records from courts, correctional facilities and some state criminal databases. The searches conducted by these companies are not based on fingerprints. They are based on name, date of birth and Social Security numbers. Because not all states provide their criminal records to private companies, the search results will not include criminal records from every state, even if the company's search report states it is a "nationwide" check.[26]

Military Criminal History Record Checks

Many nonprofits and other community serving organizations benefit greatly from the efforts of present and former members of the armed forces. Just as with other types of applicants, organizations need to use due diligence and vet these applicants. Apply the same policies used for other applicants including checking their military criminal histories.

Organizations seeking access to military records must have the individual's personal information (name, date of birth, and Social Security number), branch of service, and a valid reason for needing the information. If the individual is on active duty, the best contact is with the Judge Advocate General Office at the base where the applicant is stationed. If the individual is a former member of the military separated within the past several years, military records must be obtained from the records custodian for the service branch in which the individual served. In order to obtain this information, the applicant must give his or her authorization. When requesting information concerning present and former military personnel, a form SF-180 (**www.archives.gov/research/order/standard-form-180.pdf**) must be submitted.

International Criminal History Records

Any foreign national entering the United States on a visa must satisfy a U.S. embassy official in his or her country of origin that the visa applicant has "Good Moral Character." However, embassy officials may not be using the same criteria as your organization. In addition, many nonprofits do not require volunteers to show proof of their residency status. The Australian Government Division of Immigration and Citizenship publishes a guide for obtaining police certificates. The February 2013 edition guide is available as a PDF document on their website (**www.immi.gov.au/Help/Pages/character-police/requirements.aspx**). This bulletin has an alphabetical listing of contacts and procedures in each country for obtaining criminal history record checks. Organizations need to be very wary of vendors stating that they perform international record checks. Ask for sources of information, countries from which records are available, and frequency of up-dates. There is no all-encompassing international criminal history database.

Driving Records

The operation of a motor vehicle is often a part of many volunteer and paid positions. Anytime a staff member—volunteer or paid—operates a vehicle on behalf of a nonprofit there is potential liability for the organization and, more importantly, the possibility of harm to the organization's clientele who may be transported in the vehicle. If there is even a remote possibility that a staff member will operate a vehicle on behalf of the organization or as a service to the organization's clientele, driving record checks need to be part of the staff screening process. In fact, some insurance companies may require them as a requirement for the organization's automobile liability insurance.

Fortunately, most background checking vendors offer this service and may include it in the package of record checks performed for your organization at a modest increase in cost. Most states charge fees of less than $5.00 to undertake the driving record checks. Your insurance company may also assist in obtaining the record checks as a service to policyholders.

Credential Verification

Many nonprofit staff positions require a credential—license, training certificate, or college diploma—to document an applicant's qualification to perform the duties of the position. For example, many caregiver positions require certification in cardio-pulmonary resuscitation (CPR). Through its chapters, the American Red Cross offers CPR training and awards certificates valid for one year after successful completion of the training. In order to verify that an applicant fulfills the prerequisites for a caregiver position the organization should:

1. Ask for a copy of the certificate or wallet card given to the individual upon completion of the course.

2. Check the date awarded and the expiration date.

3. Contact the Red Cross Chapter that gave the certificate to verify its validity.

4. If the applicant does not have a certificate or card, ask for the date of the training, the organization that provided the training, and the name of the instructor. Then follow up with that organization.

This would be the same kind of process used to verify similar kinds of credentials or licenses from the Red Cross as well as from other organizations and agencies. Remember the old adage: Trust but verify.

Academic degrees can be verified by the registrars of the institutions from which they were received. Usual information needed for verification includes the name used by the individual during their enrollment, their date of birth and social security number, the dates of attendance, the degree received and authorization by the applicant to release the information to the inquiring nonprofit.

Credential verification is also a service offered by many consumer reporting organizations. The benefits of using such a vendor includes turning the responsibility over to an entity used to obtaining such information. A good professional vetting of applicants can ensure more positive results. The down side may be that by using a consumer reporting agency, the requirements of the Fair Credit Reporting Act are triggered and it may create some delays while the requirements of the act are being implemented. Cost of the service may also be a factor in deciding to employ a credentials verification service or to use the nonprofit's staff.

Residency Status

The *Immigration Reform and Control Act (IRCA)* of 1986 prohibits employers from hiring individuals that are not entitled to be legally employed in the U.S. This includes citizens from other countries that are in this country illegally and those whose visas do not permit them to be employed in this country. Purely volunteer positions are not impacted by this legislation. Please note, however, that according to the guidance given to employers, proof of eligibility for employment must be provided anytime something of value—"remuneration"—is given in exchange for labor or services—this includes food and lodging.[27] Some positions that are thought of as volunteer positions may be covered by the provisions of this law.

The screening that employers may do prior to hiring is limited by the act and employers may face significant financial penalties if the law is violated. If the position comes under the purview of the IRCA, the organization may place a statement on the application form or in the position description that applicants must be legally entitled to be employed in the U.S. Employers may not restrict a position to U.S. citizens nor discourage applicants from specific countries from applying. Here again one must return to the position description to determine what—if any—restrictions or requirements are necessary to fulfill the demands of the position.

Documentation of applicant eligibility may not be requested until after the hire date. According to the M-274 handbook, "You may not begin the Form I-9 process until you offer an individual a job and he or she accepts your offer."[28] Employers have a limited amount of time to complete the I-9 process-usually 3 days. The M-274 Handbook for Employers is available online at **www.uscis.gov/files/form/m-274.pdf**.

The U.S. Citizen and Immigration Services agency (USCIS) also offers an e-verify program for electronically verifying employment eligibility. E-verify is offered in partnership with the Social Security Administration and also is used to verify Social Security numbers.

Social Network and Internet Searches

In a recent CareerBuilder survey, 35% of the employers in the survey admitted to using the information about a candidate that they discovered online as the primary reason for not hiring them.[29] Common reasons included:

- Provocative or inappropriate photos or information of the candidate were found online: 53 %

- Potential employee posted about personally drinking or using drugs: 44 %

- Bad-mouthing of previous employer, co-workers or clients online: 35%

- Bad grammar or communication skills: 29 %

- Discriminatory comments made: 26 %

- Discovery that the candidate lied about qualifications: 24 %[30]

The question that has yet to be resolved is, "Should employers use information from social networking sites to base employment decision on?" The argument against using such sites as Facebook, MySpace and other similar sites is that by visiting personal social media sites of applicants, an employer may learn information about applicants that cannot be used— age, sex, life-style, race, religion and disabled status—in making employment decisions. Looking at a social network page and then deciding not to hire an applicant may open the door to litigation under Title VII of the Civil Rights Act. Some would argue that using information posted on social media websites triggers the requirements of the FCRA. Since the use of such sites for screening is relatively new, not much case law has been developed around these issues although every indication from lawyers specializing in employment is that litigation is on the way.

A 2010 survey conducted by Microsoft and Cross-Tab reported that in the U.S., of surveyed recruiters and HR professionals, 75% reported that their companies have formal policies in place requiring hiring personnel to research applicants online. Such research includes a variety of information resources including search engines (78%), social media (63%), photo and video sharing sites (59%), professional and business networking sites (57%), personal websites (48%), personal blogs (46%), news sharing sites like Twitter (41%), and various other kinds of Web sources including 25% looking at posts on classified and Web auction sites including Craigslist.[31]

If your nonprofit thinks it needs to use information from social media and Internet websites, there are some guidelines that may facilitate their use:

- Be transparent. Request permission from applicants to visit their websites.

- Discuss with applicants their assessment of the usefulness of content in supporting their quest for a position. Have they 'googled' themselves to see what information comes up?

- Ask if there is any content on their webpages that would cast them in a negative light.

- Ask how the applicant uses their networks.

- Ask applicants if they have ever used their social media posts to bad-mouth their employers or fellow employees.

- Share any policies that your organization has for employee use of social network media.

- Consider how your organization will address the disparities created in the screening process if all applicants do not have social network pages.

- Have your attorney review all staff screening processes that relate to social networks and the Internet.

Recap: Keys to Record Checks

Nearly every aspect of our lives is captured and stored in some kind of record. Some of these records are intended to be very private and confidential; others are deemed to be public.

There is a disconnection between consumer feelings about appropriate of use of personal information for employment screening and the recruiters and HR professionals seeking high-quality, low-risk staff members. Most consumers accept the idea that doing an Internet search on Google and checking professional and business networks is perfectly appropriate. There is a more diverse point of view when it comes to using personal websites and video or photo sharing sites for employment screening.[32]

Nonprofits need to exercise due diligence when screening applicants. Part of exercising due diligence is to understand the current standards of care applicable to the screening process. When it comes to record checks, there is a much greater pressure on organizations to obtain as much information as possible. This is counter-balanced by laws and regulations governing applicant privacy and confidentiality—as well as fairness.

As presented in the first part of the **Staff Screening Notebook**, the position description sets the stage for each of the subsequent steps in the screening process. Legally, screening should be limited to obtaining the information necessary to evaluate an applicant's fitness for a particular position. Not all available information is relevant, and accessing some may increase your organization's exposure to liability for unfair employment practices and discrimination.

- Determine what information you need based upon the position description and your organization's policies.

- Determine how and where you will obtain the information.

- Follow federal, state and local employment screening laws.

- Seek legal guidance.

Appendix A: State Liability Laws Pertaining to Reference Checks

State	Statute	State	Statute
Alabama	None	Montana	Mont. Code §27-1-737
Alaska	Alaska Statue §09.65.160	Nebraska	None
American Samoa		Nevada	Nev. Stat. §41.755
Arizona	Arizona Revised Statues §12-1361	New Hampshire	None
		New Jersey	None
Arkansas	Arkansas Code Annotated §11-3-204	New Mexico	NM Stat §51-12-1)
California	Cal. Civil Code §47	New York	None
Colorado	Colo. Rev. Stat. §8-2-114	North Carolina	N.C. Stat. §1-539.12
Connecticut	None	North Dakota	N.D. Cent. Code §34-02-18.
Delaware	Del. Code 19 §709		
District of Columbia	None	Northern Marianas Islands	
Florida	FL Stat. §768.095	Ohio	OH Rev Code §4113.71
Georgia	GA. Code §34-1-4	Oklahoma	OK Stat. 40 §61
Guam		Oregon	Or.Stat. §30.178
Hawaii	HAW stat. §663-1-95	Pennsylvania	Pa. C.S.A. §8340.1
Idaho	IDAHO §44-201	Puerto Rico	
Illinois	ILL State. (§46/10)	Rhode Island	RI §28-6, 4-1
Indiana	IN Code Sec. 22-5-3-1	South Carolina	South Carolina Code of Laws §41-1-65
Iowa	Iowa Code §91B.2	South Dakota	SD §60-4-12
Kansas	Kan. Stat. Ann. §44-119a	Tennessee	TN Stat. Sec. 50-1-105
Kentucky	None	Texas	TX§103.001-005
Louisiana	La. Rev. Stat. Ann. §23:291	Utah	34-42-1
Maine	Me.26, §598	Vermont	None
Maryland	MD Code Proc. §5-423	Virginia	VA §8.01-46.1
Massachusetts	None	Virgin Islands	
Michigan	MI Law §453.452	Washington	None
Minnesota	MN Stat. Sec. 181.967	West Virginia	None
Mississippi	None	Wisconsin	Wis. Stat. sec. 895.487(2)
Missouri	RSMo 290.152	Wyoming	WY §27-1-113

States with no liability laws pertaining to reference checks: Alabama, Connecticut, District of Columbia, Kentucky, Massachusetts, Mississippi, Nebraska, New Hampshire, New Jersey, New York, Vermont, Washington and West Virginia.

Transition from Applicant to Staff Member

Step 8: Make the Selection Decision(s)

Step 9: Provide Training

Step 10: Complete an Introductory Period of Employment

Introduction

The ***Staff Screening Notebook*** presents a comprehensive, ten-step screening process designed to help nonprofit and other community-serving agencies select high quality staff members who are unlikely to cause harm to the organization or to an organization's clientele or other stakeholders. The first volume of the ***Notebook*** outlines the preparation steps an organization needs to take before accepting applications. Taking these steps ensures that organizational support and supervision is available and that the functions of the position have been fully defined.

Volume II of the ***Notebook*** offers detailed guidance on obtaining information from applicants. It discusses the kinds of information that organizations need and how to develop customized applications based on position descriptions. In addition *Volume II* discusses pre-employment interviews and their role in the screening process.

In *Volume III*, the need for obtaining information from sources other than the applicant is addressed. The traditional screening process includes reference checks, but in recent years, criminal history record checks and use of other information sources including social media websites has become increasingly commonplace as part of a thorough screening process.

In this volume, the on-boarding process is examined in the final three steps of the screening process. Our thesis is that screening continues even after the individual makes a successful transition from being an applicant to being a valuable member of the organization's staff. Our discussion will address the following steps:

- Evaluating applicants and making selection decisions (Step 8),

- Following up to meet the selectee's training needs (Step 9), and

- Utilizing the initial employment period as an extension of the screening process (Step 10).

Step 8:
Make the Selection Decision(s)

The initial steps of the screening process have enabled narrowing the field of applicants to your finalists. Presumably, the applicants have supplied information documenting their knowledge and skills related to the position for which they are submitting an application. The organization has reviewed the information received from the applicants, met with the applicants for interviews and gathered addition information concerning the applicants' qualifications. It is now time to make a selection based on the information at hand.

For many nonprofits, making the decision to accept an individual's application for a position seems intuitive. Often acceptance is based upon little more than an expression of interest on the part of the individual—this is especially true of volunteer positions. However, nonprofits should consider the benefits they gain from a more structured screening and selection process for both employees and volunteers.

A structured screening process helps to ensure that individuals will be appropriately placed-matching the requirements of the position with the skills, knowledge, and interests of the applicant. A structured screening process also offers a better opportunity to identify and eliminate applicants who may constitute identifiable risks to the wellbeing of vulnerable service recipients as well as threats to the organization's abilities to achieve its mission in the community.

The selection of staff members—paid or volunteer—is a serious responsibility that has consequences. Even if there were no legal requirements—and as we have shown, there are many—staff selection influences how your organization is perceived by the community you serve. The staff selection process also influences how your organization is perceived by your staff members. High caliber staffing improves your brand and your organization's ability to achieve its mission. Sloppy screening may result in the wrong people being selected thereby placing your clientele and the organization at risk.

Hopefully, you have been able to whittle down the applicant pool using logical decision points after considering applications and as you have implemented the other steps we have laid out. Before making an offer, however, it is time to step back, take a deep breath, and take a final look at the position description, the selection criteria and all of the information obtained on your finalists. Assess how well the applicants match up to the requirements of the position. What are the strengths and weaknesses of each finalist? Does each finalist meet the "must have" skills and knowledge required for the position? What about the intangible qualities that are hard to measure—desire to do the job, organizational fit, ability to grow in (and with) the organization?

Do You Feel Confident about Offering the Position to One of Your Finalists?

According to a 2012 global research report about hiring trends that was published by the management consulting firm Development Dimensions International (DDI), one in eight new workers employed during a 12-month period proved to be a bad hire causing many employers that DDI surveyed to question whether they have made wise hiring decisions.[33] If after implementing this screening process you still have doubts about the abilities of your finalists to be successful in the position, it's time to analyze the source of your discomfort:

- *Is the position structured properly? Are the functions doable? Is the compensation adequate to attract qualified candidates?* Nonprofits are often placed in quandaries. There may be a need for additional staff to handle the workload, but the demands may be in areas that make it difficult to find an individual with the skillset for performing in all of the areas of need. Sometimes we're looking for a person with extraordinary abilities that just doesn't exist. And, for some fields, nonprofits find it difficult to offer competitive compensation. If any of these factors are causing your discomfort you may need to rethink the position. Instead of one full-time staff member, you may need to consider splitting it into part-time positions. Some highly qualified individuals may prefer a part-time position that allows them time to pursue other interests or obligations. If the skills you need are specialized, you may consider looking for someone you can train—there may even be jobs-training funds available to help support the training. If monetary compensation is limited, benefit packages may be enhanced to attract the talent your organization needs.

- *Are your selected finalists unable to meet the minimum requirements?* Minimum qualifications are the very least that an individual must meet in order to obtain the position. If your applicant pool doesn't have folks who can meet the requirements—assuming that the position was properly structured—you may need to reopen the position to more applications and reconsider the strategies you use to advertise and recruit applicants. If you select an applicant who does not meet the minimums, you need a plan for how the organization can develop the selected individual's capabilities and meet the minimums within an acceptable time period.

- *Are personal bias and prejudices getting in the way of making an informed decision?* Whether we are aware of them or not, as humans we have biases and prejudices formed from our cultural and life experiences. We may need to overcome such limitations when making selection decisions to staff our organizations. It is true that irrespective of the talents an applicant has, unless he or she is able to fit into the organization in a productive manner, the placement will not be successful. One way to minimize the impact of personal bias when screening and selecting staff members is to include others in the decision making process. Such involvement may be brought about by affording qualified applicants opportunities to meet and talk with others in the organization then using feedback from these interactions to help make the final decision.

Making staffing decisions affords the opportunity for some organizational introspection. Take a good look around the organization. Does the staff reflect the make-up of the community? Are members of minority groups, individuals with disabilities, and other diverse characteristics fairly represented on the organization's staff? If the answers to these questions are negative, perhaps it's time to find out if the organization is doing all it can to reasonably attract qualified applicants with more diverse characteristics.

Making the Offer

Employees and volunteers need to receive notification that their applications to work for your organization have been accepted. Initial notification may be through telephone calls but all accepted applicants should receive written documentation of the offer.

For volunteer and employee positions, the notification letter should include a welcome to the organization and a statement about the important contribution that the staff member will make in the organization's accomplishment of its mission.

For volunteers, the letter should indicate the volunteer status of the position but explain any compensation that is associated with the position—this could include reimbursement for some expenses, parking, meals that are provided, mileage for personal car use associated with the position and any other kind of benefits your organization offers to its volunteers. The welcoming letter may also include an invitation to your organization's volunteer orientation meeting—possibly an online webinar or e-training session. Finally, the acceptance letter should request any additional information that is required such as proof of vehicle liability insurance and a copy of the volunteer's driver's license.

For paid positions, the offer letter should serve as written documentation of any and all verbal agreements reached between the applicant and the organization, including the weekly or monthly starting salary, or for non-exempt positions, the initial hourly rate of pay. It should state that the position is at will and whether it is classified as an exempt or non-exempt position. The letter should include the start date, the location to report to and the name of the person to report to. The letter should also state any conditions that are placed on the offer such as "contingent upon confirmation of legal residency."

The written offer should never be sent to the applicant's current place of employment in any form—regular mail, email, courier—unless requested by the applicant. The preferred method of delivery would be regular mail to the applicant's residence. Some organizations require that the applicant sign a copy of the offer letter for placement in the individual's personnel file.

Letters offering employment should not be lengthy. They are documentation of mutual agreements between the applicant and the organization. They do not replace the personnel policies of the organization as expressed in the organization's employee handbook. Offer letters need to be carefully checked and rechecked. If your organization commonly uses an offer of employment template, make sure that the information in it is current and not outdated. Job title, start date and compensation are particularly critical areas. A typographical error in the compensation figure could be costly. Before sending the letter, confirm that a manager will be available on the new hire's start date and has set aside time in his or her schedule to give the orientation session and introduce the new hire to other employees. If consent to follow the policies in an Employee Handbook is required of all paid staff, consider transmitting a copy of the handbook with the offer letter.

Step 9:
Provide Training

It's your staff member's first day. Are you ready for the new staff member? Is the work station ready—desk, telephone, supplies? Have the other staff members been informed of the new hire's coming on board? Are the necessary forms and other documents ready to be filled out and/or explained? You only have one chance to make a first impression on your new staff members and it's important that the first day on board conveys a sense of organizational competence.

A check list of forms and tasks will help the staff members and the supervisor keep track and ensure that nothing falls through the cracks. The check list may include:

- Payroll forms, W-2 information for state and federal taxes

- Completion of the I-9 form for Employment Eligibility Verification

- Personal information including emergency contacts

- Banking forms for direct deposit of paychecks

- Health insurance forms

- Other insurance forms included in your organization's benefits package

- A guided tour of the facility and introductions to other staff members

- Certification of receipt of the organization's staff handbook and review of the more significant policies in the handbook with the supervisor

- Signing a confidentiality agreement (if appropriate)

- Providing a copy of the staff members driver's license and proof of vehicle liability insurance

- Setting goals to be accomplished during the staff member's initial period of employment including the successful completion of any required training

- End of day debriefing to answer any questions the new staff member has

The first day that a new staff member joins your organization may be the most important day in that individual's tenure with the organization. By setting the appropriate tone in the beginning, the organization sets a standard for quality that carries over in the new staff member's attitude about the organization and the staff member's value to the organization.

Even the most qualified new staff members will probably have some training needs to adapt their skills and knowledge to your organization's methods of doing things. This training needs to begin from the first day on the job. For example, if you are a social services organization, your organization may use a proprietary computer software package to document client services. New staff members will not be fully productive until they master your organization's case management system. Learning how to use that system should be part of the training during the initial period of employment.

Many organizations pair new staff members with more experienced staff members who serve as mentors or coaches helping new comers to learn the ways your organization operates and how to fit their position responsibilities in the overall organizational structure. The selection of mentors/coaches is critical. The wrong staff member assigned to this function can result in shoddy performance and development of bad habits for the newcomer. Staff members who are assigned responsibilities for training new staff need to not only know *how* something is to supposed be done, but also *adhere to* the organization's procedures in fulfilling his or her daily duties. Veteran staff members all too often develop short cuts that fall outside of the organization's protocols—these should not be passed on to the newcomers. To ensure that staff members are learning the proper protocols, the evaluators of progress may need to be different from the coach/mentor.

Observation and frequent feedback are the keys to the new staff on-boarding process. Evaluating how well staff members reach their training goals is part of the on-going screening process that takes place after your organization makes its selection decisions. Your organization may find it useful to use a training checklist based upon the position description. Such a checklist may be used to assess the skill levels of new staff members and to develop a plan to ensure that all of the skills needed to perform the duties of the position are developed within the initial employment period.

In addition to the coach/mentor on-the-job training, some training may need to be obtained outside of the organization, for example, CPR training delivered by a local chapter of the American Red Cross or a local hospital. If this kind of training is required by the organization or is a requirement of the position, the organization should provide the time and expense necessary for a staff member to complete the training.

The training during the initial period of employment may be considered somewhat differently than on-going staff development training offered by the organization. During the initial period of employment, training is focused on ensuring that the staff member has the skills and knowledge to perform at an entry level stage for the position. Once the initial period of employment has been completed and proficiency in the position has been demonstrated, additional staff development training can enhance the skills and enable growth within the organization.

Step 10:
Complete an Introductory Period of Employment

When an organization selects an applicant for a staff position, it is making a decision to invest organizational resources in the individual to enable the individual to fulfill the responsibilities set forth in the position description. The applicant on the other hand, in accepting a position, agrees to restructure his or her life around the requirements of the organization and the position for which he or she was hired and for whatever compensation that accompanies that position. The period of time immediately after selecting a new staff member may be used by the organization to validate its selection of the staff member and to develop the new staff member into a fully functional and productive member of the organization's team.

PLEASE NOTE: This period of time should not be referred to as a "probationary period." This terminology may imply that successful completion of probation confers some special employment status—it should not, and in most states with "at will employment," it does not. The initial period of employment is a developmental period designed to provide the staff member an opportunity to become proficient in the responsibilities of the position and to provide the organization with an opportunity to structure a developmental process and evaluate the results.

The organization needs to be clear with staff members from the very beginning about the specific goals and milestones to be achieved during the initial period of employment. Such clarity avoids misunderstandings and helps to ensure working together to achieve common goals. Having a "punch list" of tasks to be addressed during the initial period of employment may help to avoid omissions of important areas of job-related skills and knowledge.

In the sense that it is a developmental period, it would be reasonable for the organization to offer increased compensation to employees who fulfill the nonprofit's expectations. The rationale for increasing compensation is that the staff member will have transitioned from a new hire with undemonstrated skills and knowledge to a more productive member of the staff.

The period of initial employment not only offers the organization an opportunity to assist new staff members to become comfortable in performing the duties of their jobs, it also offers new staff members an opportunity to self-evaluate their performance and to assess their decision to join the organization. By the conclusion of the initial period of employment, the staff member and the organization should be able reach a joint decision about their mutual compatibility and long-term prospects for a successful relationship.

A Word about Volunteers

Throughout the **Staff Screening Notebook** the emphasis may more clearly be associated with the screening of employees rather than the screening of volunteers. This section of the **Notebook** addresses specifically how to apply the 10-step screening process to volunteer staff members.

In the nonprofit sector, volunteers are critical resources upon which many organizations rely to accomplish their missions. Accomplishing organizational missions may rest more in the hands of volunteer staff members than in an organization's paid staffing. At the same time volunteers create many of the same risks for an organization that paid employees also create. Failure to adequately screen and supervise volunteers has caused significant liability claims for nonprofits and their insurers. Even without the threat of legal liability, organizations have a moral responsibility to adequately screen volunteers, especially those who will work with vulnerable service recipients—children, individuals with disabilities, and the dependent elderly.

Every volunteer working in nonprofit organizations has always had some form of screening even if that screening process was unstructured and informal. For example, "Hey Joe, you enjoy working with kids, I think you should consider becoming a mentor in our organization." This statement is a form of screening. Based on what the individual knows about Joe and Joe's interests, he's recruiting Joe to be a mentor. This kind of screening has been practiced in community-serving organizations since the first nonprofits were organized and volunteers donated their talents to assist their communities.

As the nonprofit sector became more structured, more formal screening processes were developed. This formalization of screening has been driven both by a desire to better serve service recipients as well as by a growing awareness of liability exposures within the nonprofit field. The screening process presented in the **Staff Screening Notebook** will assist nonprofit organizations to improve the quality of their services and manage the risks to service recipients and to the organization that may be created by volunteer staffers. It may also increase volunteer satisfaction by placing volunteers in positions where their contributions to the organization's success make optimum use of their knowledge and skills.

Screening and Performance Management Go Hand In Hand

One of the biggest challenges in screening is determining the need to re-screen staff members and volunteers after they begin employment. This question becomes very complicated when you consider executives and staff leaders, particularly those who have served your organization for many years. Oftentimes, these high-level and long-term staff members are given passes from continued screening; they are not re-screened because they have already earned the trust of the organization. Why do we allow these leaders to forgo additional screening when we have all heard tales of CEO embezzlements and other betrayals from trusted staff? An essential element of the screening process is that it should be implemented *consistently* and *without prejudice*. No one in your organization should be above suspicion—not even the CEO or the most dedicated volunteer.

That being said, you may not feel a need to submit these committed workers to the same type of screening year after year. For example, if you typically implement a schedule for repeated reference and background checks, you might find that this is costly over time and it does not guarantee procurement of additional helpful information. Consider using a more sophisticated, interactive screening resource for high-level and long-term staff members: performance management. Effective performance management will allow you to supervise key leaders while offering them opportunities to develop and continue their service. Consider using the strategies below to link performance management and screening.

Strategies for Using Performance Management as a Screening Resource

- Aim to hold brief, casual feedback discussions between formal performance reviews. This allows you to provide continual supervision and feedback without overwhelming key leaders.

- Address high-risk duties in performance standards and during performance reviews. When you design performance benchmarks for a staff member who has high access to financial resources, include standards for honest and transparent fiscal management. Address these areas during performance reviews to signal the employee that he or she is being supervised and screened for these potential risks.

- Use observations and results from performance reviews to inform your decisions about necessary screening. For example, if you observe a key leader falling behind or acting out of character, this may prompt you to provide additional supervision or to implement typical re-screening techniques as necessary.

The 10-Step Screening Process—Volunteer Focus

Step 1: Define the Position—Just as with paid employees, volunteer staff members need to have a written description of their assigned responsibilities. The same format suggested for use in our earlier discussion of this step may be used for volunteer positions. Nonprofit organizations also need to consider the other aspects of planning for volunteer staffing. Volunteers need supervision even if it's from other volunteers.

Inadequate planning for volunteer utilization may be one of the most common deficiencies in nonprofit administration. Inadequate planning may waste opportunities created by volunteers such as internship students seeking meaningful experience in the nonprofit sector or high school students fulfilling their community service requirements for graduation.

The driving question for all nonprofits is, "How can the organization utilize volunteers to further its abilities to carry out its stated mission?" When a nonprofit accepts offers of volunteer service, it is also accepting the responsibilities to supervise and support their activities. The volunteer position description needs to specify:

- what the volunteers will do

- who their supervisor will be

- what hours they will work

- where their duty station is located

- the knowledge and skill set that is required

Sometimes the best use for volunteers is a project or a set of tasks that once completed result in a sense of closure. Projects have defined beginning and end points and for this reason are great assignments for interns coming in for a semester or for the summer.

Another kind of volunteers that are often overlooked in the position planning process is volunteer board members. While your organization may have a nominating committee to screen and select prospective members for your board, position descriptions for board members will help the nominating committee to do its job better.

Step 2: Determine Qualifications—Most nonprofit organizations have progressed beyond the point of accepting anyone who walks through the door as a volunteer. It's possible that organizations may have more generic qualifications for volunteers than they have for paid employees, but there are some basic qualifications that volunteers need depending upon the services that they will render. Ivan Scheier, an early and innovative thinker in the volunteer field, advanced the "Min-Max" theory of volunteerism.[34] He posited that volunteers are most effective when organizations use volunteers' existing strengths. "Min-Max" is minimum change for maximum output. By developing the volunteer position description, the organization has a basis for screening individuals to take advantage of skills they bring for specific assignments.

In addition to meeting the requirements for specific positions or functions, volunteers need to also meet the general requirements for working as a volunteer in the organization. General requirements usually include character traits and criminal histories. Your organization should have a policy adopted by its governing body that sets general requirements for volunteers affiliated with your organization.

Step 3: Set the Selection Criteria—Just as with paid staff, the selection criteria should be established before trying to recruit volunteers. In addition to having the skills and knowledge for the position, other criteria could include having the time to devote, availability of reliable transportation, willingness to participate in an organizational volunteer orientation or other training, and passing the organization's background checks.

Step 4: Create the Application—Applications for volunteer positions should help an organization collect sufficient information to assess applicants and determine if they meet the minimum qualifications for the position. Items in the application should relate to the responsibilities of the position as well as the general qualifications set by the organization for all volunteers.

Laws governing employment applications do not generally apply to applications for volunteer positions, but areas of inquiry forbidden in screening potential employees should be avoided unless necessary to achieve the mission of the organization. Organizations should research state and local laws to determine what, if any, areas are off-limits to volunteer screening.

Step 5: Conduct Interviews—When recruiting volunteers, the interviewing process may begin before the application is submitted. Many organizations use groups to recruit applicants for volunteer positions. For example, the Boy Scouts of America has a "School Night for Scouting" event during which parents are asked to volunteer for various unit level positions. Big Brothers Big Sisters of America's local chapters may have a group orientation for individuals wanting to be mentors. Both of these examples help to accomplish one of the purposes of an interview and that is to provide sufficient information to a prospective volunteer to enable them to decide if volunteering might be something that they would like to do—or that they would be able to do.

Group meetings do not eliminate the need for face-to-face interviews, but they help expedite the screening process by removing from the volunteer pool individuals for whom volunteering would be unfeasible or those who are disinterested. Applicants for positions giving direct access to vulnerable individuals or to information about vulnerable individuals need to have a more in-depth interview that explores relevant experience and their motivations for volunteering.

Step 6: Check References—The failure to check references often becomes a focal point when a volunteer causes harm during the course of his or her volunteer service. It is especially important to check with organizations in which the volunteer rendered similar services for vulnerable service recipients. Some volunteers seek to offer volunteer service to organizations franchised by a specific national organization with which they may have a long history with several of the local branches. When a volunteer has served in another local nonprofit that is part of the same umbrella organization and seeks to transfer into a new local organization, it should be mandatory for information about past service be part of the screening process. It is important that references for volunteers be qualified as to direct knowledge of relevant information as discussed earlier in the *Staff Screening Notebook*.

Step 7: Conduct Background Checks—Unfortunately, volunteer screening has almost become synonymous with conducting background checks. As we emphasize here, background checks—criminal history and driving record checks—are important components of an overall comprehensive approach to screening all staff including volunteers. Record checks may be important in disqualifying applicants for volunteer positions, but they should never be considered sufficient qualification for a volunteer position. When the Catholic Church was called upon to address the molestation of young people by priests, the probability of identifying the alleged perpetrators through criminal history records was probably close to zero. However, as record checking services document, a number of volunteer applicants have criminal history records that should disqualify them from working with children.

Step 8: Make the Selection Decision—With adequate supervision available, most nonprofit and community-serving organizations welcome all qualified applicants for volunteer positions. Unfortunately, many nonprofits have client waiting lists for critical services due to shortages of volunteers. Even with the pressures of unmet demands for services, organizations are well-advised not to short-cut the screening process.

Step 9: Provide Training—Some level of training is necessary for most volunteer positions. This training may be so critical that it is mandatory. Earlier in my career, I was privileged to direct a volunteer juvenile probation officer program. I designed the training to be a part of the screening process scheduling it over several weeks for 90 minutes one night a week. In addition to the knowledge that the volunteer gained about the juvenile court and their specific do's and don'ts, part of the screening was the ability of the volunteers to pledge their time and fulfill the commitment. The juveniles they would be assigned had too many adults in their lives who failed to keep their commitments and I needed to be sure that we kept ours.

Step 10: Complete an Introductory Period of Service—During this period the organization needs to be especially alert to any signs that the volunteer needs additional support—back-up volunteers, coaching, additional training or orientation, or, in some cases, words of encouragement. If it looks like the volunteer placement is not working out, a candid discussion with the volunteer may assist in making a mutual decision about the volunteer's future—or lack thereof—with the organization. Termination of a volunteer may be necessary, but unless there is a serious allegation of criminal conduct such as child sexual abuse, it can be done in ways that allows the volunteer to maintain good feeling about the organization and its mission.

Nonprofit organizations can reinforce volunteers' commitments to service by recognizing volunteer achievement. While the purpose of the initial period of service is to ensure that the volunteer understands his or her role within the organization, a simple certificate in an inexpensive frame documenting the acceptance of the individual as a volunteer in the organization is almost always appreciated.

Self-Screening

Although most staff screening activity is initiated by staff at a nonprofit, self-screening is initiated by a prospective applicant. Aspects of self-screening should be part of your application—certain questions may dissuade an applicant from throwing her "hat in the ring." Keep in mind that anything you can do to help prospective applicants determine whether they are a good match for your open staff or volunteer roles potentially saves your organization the time and financial resources necessary for screening.

Below is a wonderful example of a self-screening tool for volunteer roles—a list of Volunteer FAQs. This list is featured on the website of the New England Aquarium (www.neaq.org/get_involved/volunteering_and_internships/volunteering/Volunteer_FAQs.php). It is featured here with permission. When developing a list of FAQs for your website, consider including questions that address:

- Questions frequently asked by prospective and new volunteers

- Common misconceptions about volunteer or staff roles at your nonprofit

- Information helpful to understand your nonprofit's culture or environment

VOLUNTEER FAQS

The Aquarium would not be able to operate without the help of its volunteers. Volunteering has great rewards, but it's also a big commitment. Find out if volunteering at the New England Aquarium is right for you. Below are answers to several frequently asked questions.

Is there a time commitment for volunteering?

Are there volunteering opportunities that are shorter than six months?

I only want to volunteer for the summer, what positions are available?

Do volunteer positions have age restrictions?

Are there volunteer opportunities for teens and high school students?

Can I do my senior project at the New England Aquarium?

Do you have volunteer opportunities on the weekends?

Do you have opportunities for group volunteering?

When is the best time to apply?

What is your selection process for volunteers and how competitive is it?

What is the difference between volunteering and interning?

I am currently job searching and have a lot of free time—can I volunteer?

Is there a waitlist that I can join?

Will you notify me if there's an opening?

Do you keep my application on file?

Can I dive in the Giant Ocean Tank as a volunteer?

Can volunteering lead to job opportunities?

I want to volunteer in your Animal Care Center in Quincy, MA. Do I need to have access to a car?

I am a former volunteer; how do I get involved again?

Screening Paid versus Volunteer Staff: What's the Difference?

	Paid Staff	Volunteer Staff
Legal Risks	Exposure to claims alleging: • Negligent Screening / Selection • Discriminatory Screening	Exposure to claims alleging: • Negligent Screening / Selection NOTE: with rare exception, volunteers are not protected under federal and state anti-discrimination laws. The exceptions are: • When the volunteer is serving as a condition of receiving welfare assistance or benefits • When the volunteer receives significant remuneration or benefits (such as insurance coverage, retirement benefits, etc.) • When the volunteer role is a precursor to a paid position in the organization or gives the individual a substantial advantage in being considered for a paid position
Position Description	A job description or position description is the foundation for effective screening. At a minimum, a job description should contain: • Position Title • Reporting Relationship • Supervisory Role, if applicable (e.g., 4 direct reports) • Exempt or Non-Exempt designation • Full-time or Part-time status • Reference to at-will or contract status • Eligibility for Benefits • Qualities (e.g., sense of humor, problem-solving skills) • Educational and licensing requirements • Duties and Responsibilities	A volunteer position description is key to effective volunteer recruitment and screening. At a minimum, a position description for a volunteer role should contain: • Position title or role (e.g., Board Member, Volunteer Tour Guide, Volunteer Tutor) • Reporting relationship • Supervisory Role, if applicable • Clear and repeated references to the volunteer nature of the role • Duties and responsibilities

	Paid Staff	Volunteer Staff
Selection Criteria	Clear screening criteria based on the needs of the organization, the educational and experience requirements for the position, and criteria based on the risks of position (e.g., Day Care Lead Teacher—applicants with prior convictions for any crime involving the abuse or neglect of children are ineligible for this position).	Clear screening criteria based on requirements and risks of position— volunteer screening should be more than a background check! For example: Volunteer Driver—applicants with prior DUI convictions are ineligible for consideration.
Application	Ask only questions that can and will be used to legally screen applicants. In general, do not ask questions related to: • Age or birthdate • High school graduation date • Family or marital status (e.g., married? Do you have children?) • Disabled status • Prior arrest record NOTE: a relatively recent trend is what is referred to as "ban the box laws." As of this writing, 12 states have adopted ban the box laws which prohibit certain employers from including a question about prior criminal convictions on the initial application for employment. For more information, see page 46.	Research state and local laws to determine what areas are off-limits for volunteer screening.
Interview	Formal interview.	Pre-interview interaction (e.g., initial volunteering opportunity), followed by interview.

	Paid Staff	Volunteer Staff
Criminal History Record Check	If you retain a third-party vendor to conduct criminal history record checks, seek assurance that your vendor adheres to Fair Credit Reporting Act (FCRA) standards. Other requirements and laws may apply to background checks performed by the organization through state criminal history record repositories.	Complete criminal history record checks for high-risk positions. In July 2011, the **Federal Trade Commission (FTC)** issued an expanded and more liberal interpretation of the FCRA's language: *employment purposes.* Under the new interpretation, FCRA compliance rules apply to both paid and volunteer positions. To comply with the FCRA, make certain that you: 1. Obtain consent prior to the background check; 2. Notify the applicant of negative information before taking any adverse action; 3. Notify the applicant of his/her right to a copy of the report; 4. Notify the applicant of his/her right to appeal any action; and 5. Properly dispose of information received in the report.
Reference Check	Always check references! Request relevant references for the position. Ask the applicant if there are any reasons (and if so, why), a current or former employer should not be contacted for a reference.	Always check references! Request references from prior paid and volunteer roles, and don't discount personal references. Many nonprofits report receiving candid and useful information from personal reference sources!

	Paid Staff	Volunteer Staff
Training	Offer a structured training period with a timeline for follow-up. Ensure the employee has a clear understanding of specific training requirements for the position. Discuss employer/employee responsibility for any follow-up and ongoing training associated with the position.	Volunteer onboarding and orientation is essential. Depending on the volunteer role, the orientation may cover fewer topics than an employee orientation. For some volunteer roles it may make sense to offer a series of orientation sessions, each covering a specific topic. And for some volunteer roles, such as board member, an orientation session on a single day involving all new members, may be the best approach. This all-hands style of orientation provides an opportunity for volunteers to get to know one another, as well as the organization.
Introductory Period of Employment	Formal introductory period of employment. Schedule a review after the initial employment period to determine if both the employer and employee are in agreement about whether the position is a good match for the employee and the nonprofit.	Introductory period of service. Look for signs showing that the volunteer needs more training or support.

A Final Word

Twenty years ago, the Nonprofit Risk Management Center published the first edition of the *Staff Screening Toolkit*. In the ensuing time, there have been many developments in screening staff members for community serving organizations. For example, twenty years ago, processing a criminal history record check may have taken months. Today, with many third-party vendors, the availability of this information is nearly instantaneous. Google and Facebook open applicants' lives to a level of scrutiny never before imagined. A recent story in *The Washington Post* discussed the use of online tests as a pre-interview screening tool. A growing number of organizations require applicants to complete and pass a test before they select applicants for interviews. These tests may focus on aptitude, skills or competencies, or they may be personality tests intended to gauge applicant personalities and behaviors in the workplace. The overall goal of pre-employment testing seems to be determining whether an applicant: can do the job, will do the job, and is a good fit for the organization's culture.

Many years of litigation centered around claims of negligent screening offers additional insight to shape current and future screening practices in nonprofit organizations. Legal claims and their results have influenced perceived standards of care and have arguably forced nonprofits to become more sophisticated in the screening of all staff members—paid and volunteer.

There is little doubt that in the next two decades, staff screening will continue to evolve with technological developments and legal risk continuing to be primary driving forces in the field's evolution. With these two very different disciplines influencing the evolution of screening practices, it is hard to envision exactly what staff screening will look like in 20 years. One aspect of screening in the future is certain however: tomorrow's nonprofit organizations will continue to need tools, resources and insight in order to achieve the two primary goals of any screening process: finding the most suitable candidate for an open position, and eliminating from consideration any applicant whose background poses a danger to the organization itself or the vulnerable clients it serves.

Endnotes

1. ABA Center on Children and the Law, Washington, DC, 1995 (study funded by the Office of Juvenile Justice and Delinquency Prevention, U.S. Department of Justice, 92–MC–CX–0013).

2. Guidelines for the Screening of Persons Working With Children, the Elderly, and Individuals With Disabilities in Need of Support. 1998, NCJ 167248 (52 pp.).p. 5.

3. http://chickensoupforyoursoul.blogspot.com/2008/07/10-key-employee-attributes.html

4. www.eeoc.gov/eeoc/foia/letters/2011/title_vii_epa_information_collection.html

5. http://usatoday30.usatoday.com/money/industries/health/story/2012-01-03/health-care-jobs-no-smoking/52394782/1

6. www.eeoc.gov/policy/docs/accommodation.html

7. www.osha.gov/SLTC/workplaceviolence/

8. www.nolo.com/legal-encyclopedia/discrimination-against-the-unemployed.html

9. www.laborlawyers.com/files/28198_California%20State%20Law%20Booklet%20(March%202011).pdf. P.4.

10. State and federal laws may limit the time frame for which a criminal conviction may be requested, usually 5 to 7 years.

11. The generic use of abuse could refer to either child or elderly abuse and could be made more specific on the application to reflect the requirements of the position.

12. www.forbes.com/sites/edwardlawler/2013/03/11/job-interviews-users-beware/

13. http://guides.wsj.com/management/recruiting-hiring-and-firing/how-to-conduct-interviews/

14. www.princeton.edu/hr/policies/employment/2.2/2.2.4

15. The updates reflect the transfer of much of the responsibility for interpreting the FCRA from the Federal Trade Commission (FTC) to the newly created Consumer Financial Protection Bureau (CFPB).

16. www.mofo.com/six-states-now-require-social-security-number-protection-policies-12-09-2008/

17. Ibid.

18. www.ncjrs.gov/App/Publications/abstract.aspx?ID=254445

19. www.preventelderabuse.org/nexus/bgchecks.html [From nexus, Volume 7, Issue 2, September 2001]

20. www.lexisnexis.com/risk/newsevents/press-release.aspx?Id=1334098202928795

21. http://www.eeoc.gov/laws/guidance/arrest_conviction.cfm#IIIB

22. www.ojjdp.gov/pubs/guidelines/appen-b2.html

23. www.fbi.gov/about-us/cjis/criminal-history-summary-checks/state-identification-bureau-listing

24. www.ncjrs.gov/pdffiles1/bjs/grants/237253.pdf. p. glossary viii.

25. www.shrm.org/publications/hrmagazine/editorialcontent/pages/0102agn-employment.aspx

26. www.safetocompete.org/SoundPractices Website sponsored by the National Center for Missing and Exploited Children.

27. M-274, Handbook for Employers, U.S. Citizenship and Immigration Services. (April 30, 2013) p. 3.

28. Ibid. p. 3.

29. www.careerbuilder.com/share/aboutus/pressreleasesdetail.aspx?id=pr519&sd=8/19/2009&ed=12/31/2009

30. www.social-networking-success.com/employee-screening.html

31. www.slideshare.net/duckofdoom/dpd-online-reputation-research-overview

32. Ibid. p. 4.

33. www.shrm.org/hrdisciplines/staffingmanagement/Articles/Pages/Employers-Employees-Question-Hiring-Decisions.aspx (February 28, 2013)

34. From the author's notes from a conference conducted by Dr. Scheier at the the National Information Center on Volunteers in Courts, Denver, CO. 1974. Dr Sheier died in 2008.